Shklovsky: Witness to an Era

# Shklovsky: Witness to an Era

## SERENA VITALE

### TRANSLATED BY
### JAMIE RICHARDS

DALKEY ARCHIVE PRESS
CHAMPAIGN • LONDON • DUBLIN

Originally published in Italian as, *Viktor Šklovskij Testimone di un'Epoca* by Editori Riuniti, Rome, 1979
Copyright © 1979, 2010 by Serena Vitale
Translation copyright © 2012 by Jamie Richards
First edition, 2012

Library of Congress Cataloging-in-Publication Data

Shklovskii, Viktor, 1893-1984.
  [Sklovskij: testimone di un'epoca. English]
  Shklovsky : witness to an era / Serena Vitale ; translated by Jamie Richards.
    p. cm.
  Includes bibliographical references.
  ISBN 978-1-56478-791-0 (pbk. : alk. paper)
  1. Shklovskii, Viktor, 1893-1984--Interviews. 2. Authors, Russian--Interviews. I. Vitale, Serena. II. Richards, Jamie. III. Title.
  PG3476.S488Z46 2012
  891.73'42--dc23
  [B]
                                            2012029352

Partially funded by a grant from the Illinois Arts Council, a state agency

www.dalkeyarchive.com

Printed on permanent/durable acid-free paper and bound in the United States of America

Cover photo: V. Slavinsky

Cover: design and composition by Aaron Kerner and Susan Davis

# Contents

FRIENDSHIP. THE FUTURIST EVENINGS—
THE TECHNIQUE OF SCANDAL. BAUDOUIN
DE COURTENAY. POETS SHOULDN'T BE AL-
LOWED TO DIVORCE. SEMINARIANS AND
CARPENTERS DUKING IT OUT ON THE ICE.

## December 26

YOUNG PHILOLOGISTS MEET AND DIS-
CUSS LITERATURE AT THE UNIVERSITY
OF PETERSBURG. THE BIRTH OF FORMAL-
ISM. LEV JAKUBINSKY. YEVGENI POLI-
VANOV. POETRY AND TIME: "THE BRONZE
HORSEMAN." POETRY AS THE "DEEP JOY
OF RECOGNITION." SHKLOVSKY, SAYS
BLOK, UNDERSTANDS EVERYTHING. YURY
TYNYANOV. BORIS EIKHENBAUM. HOW
TWO EX-FORMALISTS ARGUED THE DAY
AKHMATOVA DIED. DERZHAVIN'S ARRIVAL
SPELLS THE END OF FORMALISM. MAN'S
DESTINY IS THE MATERIAL OF ART. WHICH
HAS TO BE SHAKEN UP ONCE IN A WHILE,
LIKE A CLOCK THAT STOPS TICKING. ON
THE FUTILITY OF LOOKING AT FLAGS.

Tolstoy left for the Caucasus with
an English dictionary, a flute, *The
Count of Monte Cristo*, and a samovar. An ancestor of ours left out
of *Zoo, or Letters Not about Love*.
Frightening, poetic dreams. What
does realism mean?

The word. Poetry of words and poetry
of letters. Mayakovsky loved the radio. An ugly, stupid box. One mustn't
fear the future. Tolstoy gets edited.
The old scholasticism and the new.
The living Russian word.

# Preface to the First Edition

The winter of 1978, in Russia, was among the coldest of the century. That late December in Moscow, no one spoke of anything else—on the metro, in the offices, in the shops. Little old men and women, emerging from their capsules of frozen vapor, discussed it incessantly: when had it ever been this cold? In 1915, '17, '25?

This was a question I could put to Viktor Shklovsky, to his eighty-six-year-old memory, witness to so many climates, meteorological and otherwise, as I told myself on my way to his house for the first time.

I wait a few minutes in his book-crammed study, one of the two rooms that make up the writer's home. On a massive walnut table, haphazardly stacked, Plato, Mayakovsky, Tolstoy, books on semiotics, on structuralism. Finally, preceded by the remarkably kind and ever attentive lady of the house, Serafima Gustavovna (Shklovsky's second wife), the "patriarch" makes his grand entrance, swathed in a stately, impeccable robe, outfitted with a beret for the cold and a cane for support—his steps are a bit labored, but there's a twinkle in his eye.

We introduce ourselves. Then, the formalities: I begin reading the publisher's contract, which Shklovsky has to sign for the interviews. He listens attentively to my translations of the usual clauses, and, with sublime naïveté, seriously considers each one. After a few minutes he begins to roar: Why should he grant rights for fifty years? Who are these alleged "heirs" it talks about? What "television or film use" would ever be made of this book? How can anyone write a book in ten days (the amount of time I had proposed)? After a while of this, his indignation draws upon the cautionary tales of literary history: this is a binding contract, like the ones Stellovsky ruined Dostoyevsky with . . . Never in a million years! A television crew that, unfortunately, has chosen this same day to film Shklovsky at work, comes in and stands frozen in the doorway. Shklovsky's contentious temper has been unleashed, and the hapless camera crew has walked right into it. They try in vain to camouflage themselves among the books. "Young man," Shklovsky yells, "have you read Pushkin? People need to read our classics more often . . ."

When I finally manage to get a word in, explaining that it's a standard contract, that he wouldn't have to write a book but simply answer my questions, granting me two or three hours a day, the situation begins to improve. The next day, the irate patriarch is already tame, even sweet at times . . .

After a few days, when I had told him about my work, about the authors I love and study, he was already calling me a "dear friend" and saying that he was happy about these meetings of ours (every day from one to three) because he—the "madman of letters and raving orator," as he described himself—was energized by having someone to talk to.

After our official conversations, we would keep talking, with the tape recorder off—about everything, everyday problems, the situation in Italy, Russia, about family, old and faraway friends, film, literature, the new Pope . . . In fact, in those moments it was the interviewee asking the questions: What's happening with . . . ? What are people saying about . . . ? His curiosity was voracious. Shklovsky was like an eighty-six-year-old boy.

Once in a while, when he was the one talking, old wounds would be reopened, tapping into a well of private memories, difficult experiences, regrets, and bitterness that I, by that time welcomed in their home as a friend, now keep just for myself.

We became friends.

I treasure the memory of these "off the record" chats we shared during our ritual coffee (Shklovsky delighted like a child at the opportunity—offered by my presence— to take a break from his no-coffee diet) in the "second" room; while in his work room, amid the sundry wall decorations, hung a wonderful photo of Shklovsky and Mayakovsky in neck-high bathing suits, and a portrait of Osip Mandelstam.


Why an interview with Viktor Shklovsky? The idea, when it was suggested to me, appealed immediately. It would be a chance to fill in some of the gaps in the (albeit plentiful) autobiographical writing left by Shklovsky, witness to an era that never ceases to fascinate me and that always offers new ideas for reflection and research.

I also wanted to research the significance and the effect of the division of Shklovsky into two images, which are radically distant in time and seemingly irreconcilable. First of the image of the "father" of formalism—as he is often, perhaps too hastily, described—yet also its "enfant terrible," the enthusiastic comrade who was a part of so many of the projects of the Russian avant-garde, the unconventional witness, the witty essayist, the irresistible polemicist; and second, of formalism's apostate, its "turncoat"—or, according to another point of view, of the nice old man who'd finally gotten his head on straight by returning to a non-heretical reading of the classics.

I hope the interviews demonstrate a continuity between these two images. Regardless, I believe they show that the Shklovsky of today still possesses the same felicity of reading, an extraordinary ability to physically traverse a literary text, to get inside it, to live with it. And he possesses the same "energy of delusion" that, in his time, made him an extraordinarily versatile writer (yet perhaps also kept him from developing some of his brilliant insights, or following through to all their possible conclusions), and that today, combined with the wisdom of age and a wealth of experience, translates into a new literary genre: incessant critical commentary—almost automatic

15

critical writing—somewhere between pure chatter and a series of aphorisms.

Today more than ever, the dominant feature of Shklovsky's style—no matter the form or genre—is digression, where his old love for Sterne intertwines with the unpredictable fitfulness of a feverishly exhaustive memory. And so, after vain attempts to make him "respect" my questions, I let Shklovsky give in to the almost material flow of his thoughts and memories. Some of what he says in these interviews has already been written in his books; for those already familiar with them, for devotees, it will be interesting to follow the rhythm of these new associations and combinations, to notice the additions, revisions, omissions. As for me, I did everything possible to fit all of it into the book, restricting myself to removing overly obvious repetitions and moving certain blocks of the conversation to follow a thematic and chronological order, albeit a loose one. As the reader will notice, my questions often go unanswered or meet with unexpected, out-of-place responses. Eventually, I resigned myself to using the questions not as a means of finding something out, but as a technique of provocation or a springboard.

I regret that it wasn't possible to completely reproduce

the *skaz*, the "gesturality" of Shklovsky's speech: the interjections, the meaningful pauses, the muttering, the exclamations, the reconsiderations, the emptiness and the fullness of certain words. And the hearty, innocent laughter, or the sudden tears when he recalled episodes from the life (or death) of "Volodya" Mayakovsky, of "Sereza" Esenin, his formalist friends, by now almost all deceased. About that, a "technical" detail: the cold, which made the voltage vacillate wildly all over Moscow, destroyed perhaps the most precious part of the recording, containing Shklovsky's memories of his fellow Opoyazites, of the not-so-easy lot of those longstanding, courageous companions in struggle and inquiry.

It was a random accident. A stroke of bad luck. A consequence of the cold.

S.V.

MILAN, MAY 16, 1979

# New Preface
## or
## A Preface Not about the KGB


Winter 1978–79: the coldest of the century, they said, except maybe the one in '39. In Moscow, in late December, in the middle of the day, the temperature was as low as -20°C. Everyone in the streets was enveloped in little white clouds of vapor, the heating pipes had burst in many buildings, local authorities advised children and the elderly to stay in their homes. And on the morning of December 22, I went to the home of the eighty-six-year-old Viktor Shklovsky to finish making arrangements for the interviews he had agreed to do with me, out of which I planned to make a short book.

"You're going to see Shklovsky?" many Russian friends asked me in amazement, with a touch of disdain, as if I were going to bring carnations to Lenin's mummy. They hadn't forgiven him for publicly renouncing his ingenious, tumultuous origins, for giving in; they looked down on his later work—the literary theory, memoirs, critical essays:

"He's repeating himself." "But," I protested (unsuccessfully), "he wrote *Zoo, or Letters Not about Love* . . . But he was the one who helped Mandelstam when everyone else had shunned him like he was a leper . . . Growing old isn't a crime."

"Where are you going?" asked the old woman in charge of the elevator (and surveillance), popping out of her little basement room and blocking my way. "To see Shklovsky." "He's busy right now." "But I have an appointment." She checked my identification and let me go.

"You've come at a delicate moment, the TV people are here. They were late and my husband is going out of his mind," said Serafima Gustavovna Shklovskaya, helping me with my fur coat, hat, scarf, and various layers of jackets and sweaters. I could hear shouting inside. "How old are you, sonny? . . . I worked with Pudovkin, with Eisenstein, and you want to show *me* how to pose in front of the camera?" I peeked in from the foyer: almost concealed by the tall stacks of books on the table (other piles on the floor obliged the crew to move carefully through the small room), his shiny bald head shielded by a beret, checkered flannel slippers on his feet, Shklovsky was shaking his cane at the hapless crew members. "You're giving me orders like a corporal does with new recruits. *Profil! En-face . . . !* I look better in three-quarter profile. 'With a quarter-turn, oh sorrow, you look back at the indifferent.' . . . Who wrote those lines? Mandelstam. Do you know who he was, at least?" At that, the crew excused themselves from the interrogation: "All right, Viktor Borisovich, we're done!" They said good-bye; the cameraman went out into the hall and whispered to another member of the crew: "He's gone completely senile!" and to me: "Watch out! He's in a mood today."

We moved to the bedroom, which also served as a living room and dining room. Shklovsky sank into an armchair and slowly read through the Russian copy of the contract. "Worthy of Stellovsky!" he exclaimed. "You know who he is?" Fortunately, I did: Dostoyevsky's money-grubbing editor . . . And it was Anna Akhmatova looking back at the indifferent in Mandelstam's poem. He looked at me with astonishment. "Well . . . I'm impressed!" But then: "A book in less than two weeks? Impossible. I'll never do it." Hoping to appease him, I said: "But you dictated *Zoo* in nine days . . ." "True, but you're no Anna Snitkina, let alone an Elsa Triolet!" He had a point. "Grant rights for fifty years? You know how old I am?" "Those are standard provisions, Viktor Borisovich." "Learn to renew your conventions, you automatons! Fine, I'll give you a day, and then we'll see." I returned to my hotel, my body frozen and my spirits dampened—dealing with Shklovsky wasn't going to be easy. He'd been the enfant terrible, the loose cannon of formalism, he was made the protagonist of a novel called *Skandalist*—rabble-rouser, troublemaker. You couldn't say that the years had mellowed him, that's for sure. But now, that menacing, thunderous tone, like a despot's, those outbursts . . .

I returned the following day (the guard/attendant: "Where are you going?" "To see Shklovsky." "Ah."), armed with patience and a tape recorder. If it was all right with him, I explained to Viktor Borisovich, my questions would more or less go in chronological order. That was fine, he grumbled. We began with his youth, the stir caused by the emergence of formalism, the revolution, the war, Persia, the clandestine fight between the different factions of socialist revolutionaries, duels, his escape to Finland, then Berlin, his return to Russia. He would say: "I've already written about that" or "I don't know, I can't remember anymore." Or talk about something else entirely. Or out of the blue: "You know how an armored car is made?" and without waiting for my probable "no," he started going on with obscure information about turrets, machine guns, combat chambers . . . He was still a master of digression. We could continue, he told me, as our first day of work came to a close.

"Where are you going?" "To see Shklovsky." "Again?" "Yes . . ."

That day, I took the flattery approach: "Viktor Borisovich, today you're an icon, you've regained the renown you once had—" He didn't let me finish. "The only thing I need to be fully appreciated is death. Actually, maybe that's what other people need, I don't need anything." Gathering my courage, I asked about the past: What did he think now, almost forty years later, of his 1931 "Monument to a Scientific Error" in which he recanted formalism? "Important discoveries can come from an error that is opportunely revealed and taken to its logical extremes." Not another word. Moreover, many of his short, sibylline responses tended toward the aphoristic: "I never had talent, just displaced fury"; "There are only two ways to survive: write for yourself and earn money from some other occupation, or lock yourself in your house and contemplate the meaning of existence. There is no third way. I chose the third." I wondered whether these were spontaneous quips or if he had a whole repertoire prepared—to impress his audience, to avoid the more uncomfortable questions.

After three days, his elusive store of knowledge began to show itself: he must have gotten tired of playing the role of the angry Patriarch. And his voracious curiosity got the better of his reticence. Now he was the one asking me questions: on the Red Brigades ("Will there be a revolution? God save you!"), on President Pertini, on the Polish Pope . . . And what was the name of that Roman trattoria where he'd gone with that great poet, the one who was also a director? . . . "Sima!" he called his wife, who was usually sitting with us—"What was his name?" "Who, Pasolini?" "That's it. The trattoria was on one of the central streets, actually it was on a piazza. It was excellent. And I was so astonished: there were open bottles of wine on the shelves and nobody took them. And there wasn't a single drunk around . . . But you have to know it, it had a beautiful name." I improvised: "Osteria da Vittorio." "Vittorio? I think you're trying to trick poor old Viktor . . ." Then, quoting Pushkin: "It's not difficult to deceive me! Yet I'm glad to be deceived." He broke into laughter. While the sheet of ice that held Moscow hostage had reached eighty centimeters, the one between us was finally beginning to crack. I was able to confess my love for his explosive, spare writing (though I didn't mention that I'd particularly admired it in his early work). The term "parataxis" slipped out of my mouth: "*Parataksis?* What the devil is that? A pair of taxis? Or basset hounds (*taks*)?" He laughed some more. "I write short sentences out of laziness . . . And also because they don't risk being cut by the censors . . . One of them said to me—it must have been 1925, they still published me then—that my work gave them no satisfaction . . . Other writers, however . . ." "About other writers, Viktor Borisovich—what do you think of so-and-so's latest novel?" "Nothing. Because, among other things, he's one of my neighbors and he might be able to hear us. You see, a hundred and forty writers live in this building. They put us all together to keep an eye on us more easily. Like in *1984*, except that instead of television screens we have elevator patrols . . . You know, I believe I'll make it to the year 1984 . . . I would like that. I want to live. Even though I've lost all my contemporaries . . ."

"Sima" (Shklovsky's second wife—a diminutive old woman with hunched shoulders and dull eyes; she had been, people said, a stunning woman) began inviting me to have tea afterward; sometimes they even asked me to stay for dinner. Forgetting the interview, and perhaps even me—I switched off the tape recorder for discretion's sake—Viktor Borisovich gave himself over to his memories. They went back far, to painful places where self-censorship had long dictated the rules; at times his voice would crack or get stuck in his chest only to emerge, with difficulty, in a barely perceptible murmur. And more than once tears came to his eyes.

"In 1933, Gorky decided to show writers and journalists the canal that was going to connect the White Sea and the Baltic Sea, so that they could sing the praises of this great accomplishment of the new Soviet state. A grand, colossal work, a dream of Peter the Great's, and the new slaves building it were all prisoners, some of them political prisoners. I knew that my brother was among them; I eagerly accepted the invitation to see that 'creative mission.' We set off in a group of over a hundred and twenty— illustrious figures and others not so illustrious, practically unknown. They drove us far and wide, encouraged us to talk to the prisoner-workers—mostly common criminals with short sentences to serve. They all claimed to be happy that they could rehabilitate themselves through work. For at least a few weeks, in anticipation of our visit, they had been given more substantial food than their usual meager rations. For us, there was an unbelievable spread—sturgeons with sprigs of parsley in their mouths, roasted pig, sausage, ham, cheese. And bottles of vodka, wine, champagne, Borjomi water. That banquet—while the Great Famine raged in the South—took away my appetite the whole time I was writing for *Belomorkanal*, a collective work, very instructive . . . But you won't find it in the library, I don't even have a copy myself. The book was taken out of circulation as soon as it came out: in the meantime Yagoda had already been taken out and some authors had died as well—not of natural causes, you understand: Jasensky, Sviatopolk-Mirsky, Averbakh . . .

"They only let us see the inmates who had been prepared for the meeting, but with a few trinkets from Moscow I managed to unearth my brother." "Nikolai?" "What are you talking about! Nikolai was executed in 1919 . . . My brother Vladimir, a great philologist. He knew thirty languages. He translated *De vulgari eloquentia*. I learned so many things from him. He was a deeply religious man. He knew the camps—he was in Solovki from '22 to '25 . . .

When they arrested him, in 1929, he was working for Academician Marr. We hadn't been in contact for ages; he knew he was the object of keen interest on the part of the GPU and didn't want to put me in jeopardy—you know, with my history. I held back tears when I saw him. I whispered: 'Do you recognize me?' 'No,' he replied, in a firm voice—he was afraid for me. Or of me? I gave him a pack of cigarettes; he accepted them, he said, for his companions . . . The guard who had escorted me asked: 'And now, how do you feel after your reunion?' 'Like a live fox in a fur shop' . . . I never found out the day, or even the year, of his death. They arrested him again (for the seventh time) in '39 and after that I didn't hear anything. They told me he had been sentenced to ten years in the camp without the right to correspondence: at the time no one dared imagine what was hidden in that sinister phrase. I should have realized—the dead can't write. He died in 1938—I only found out after he had joined the ranks of the 'posthumously recovered.' But I still don't know where he's buried." He took a sip of water. "It's a horror, isn't it? Old people crying. It puts me off too."

"Where are you going?" "To see Shklovsky." "Again?" . . .

Proud that Viktor Borisovich had placed his trust in me, pleased that he addressed me as "Serenochka," I ventured: "How would you explain why the younger generations consider you a writer, so to speak, of the establishment?" His face drained, his stern and forbidding Dantonesque voice returned, and he shook his cane at me. "Get out of here!" he yelled. That same evening, he called to apologize.

"Where are you going?" "To see Shklovsky." "You're working today too?" "No, I just have to ask for forgiveness." The elevator attendant shrugged.

"I wrote so much just to survive. I've written mediocre, even terrible things. There's only one thing future generations will never find my name on: reports and denunciations. You must certainly think I'm a very healthy man, given that I've reached such a ripe old age. I have to disappoint you: I've been ill so often in the last thirty years that I should have been put underground long ago. My health got worse, for example, when they called meetings to expose, to censure a fellow writer. I wasn't always able to get out of them. Nor did I always want to. In '43, I too defined Zoshchenko's *Before Sunrise* as a work not 'in accordance with the interests of the people.' Zoshchenko, my pupil, one of my Serapion 'brothers.' And when they gave Pasternak the Nobel I happened to be in Yalta. I sent him a telegram with my congratulations. But then the storm broke: a 'traitor for the foreigner's coin,' they called him. And I wrote a letter to the editor at a small local newspaper allying myself with the general indignation. Why? The most terrible thing is that I don't remember anymore. The times? Sure, but we're the times, I am, millions like me. One day everything will come to light: the records of those meetings, the letters from those years, the interrogation procedures, the denunciations—everything. And all that sewage will also dredge up the stench of fear."

"Where are you going?" "To see Shklovsky." "But what-all do you have to say to each other?" I brushed off the old busybody.

Viktor Borisovich Shklovsky died in December of 1984. Recently a letter surfaced that he wrote to try to save one of his students at the Literature Institute, Arkady Belinkov, who was arrested in 1944 at twenty-three for the manuscript of *Chernovik Chuvstv* (A Notebook of Feelings), the novel he wrote for his thesis. Shklovsky wrote to the powerful writer Aleksey Tolstoy, the "Red Count," knowing that every letter sent to him was read at the Lubyanka first; his intervention saved the young man from execution, and he was only (only!) sentenced to eight years in the gulag. And in '49 he appealed to the writer

Konstantin Simonov, secretary of the Writers' Union, advocating a commutation of Belinkov's sentence: "This is a person of talent. Literary talent is not very common, people who possess it shouldn't be wasted . . ." There's a hint of goodness there, in those old papers.

### From the Record of Case no. 71/50

*Interrogation of February 15, 1944. Begun at 10:00 A.M. Concluded at 10:30 P.M.*

**Investigator**: When did you meet Shklovsky?

**Belinkov**: In July or August of 1943.

**Investigator**: Under what circumstances?

**Belinkov**: The Literature Institute encouraged us to consult writers for advice on our work.

**Investigator**: Why did you choose Shklovsky?

**Belinkov**: Because he's my favorite writer.

**Investigator**: What was Shklovsky's opinion of your *A Notebook of Feelings*?

**Belinkov**: He didn't consider it a success, but he did not say that it contained anti-Soviet material.

**Investigator**: Did you let Shklovsky in on your anti-Soviet ideas?

**Belinkov:** Yes, I did.

**Investigator:** How did Shklovsky react when you revealed these ideas?

**Belinkov:** He criticized them.

**Investigator:** Are you certain of that?

**Belinkov:** I'm certain.

**Investigator:** Did Shklovsky systematically declare his anti-Soviet views on literature and the world?

**Belinkov:** I repeat, when he spoke with me, Shklovsky never indulged in any anti-Soviet criticism.

*Interrogation of April 12, 1944. Begun at 10:30 A.M. Concluded at 5:00 P.M.*

**Investigator:** How did you meet and become acquainted with the writer Shklovsky?

**Belinkov:** In late May or early June 1943, when I was finishing at the Literature Institute and preparing to present my thesis, I was obliged to consult the writer Shklovsky for advice on my thesis, which consisted of the novel *A Notebook of Feelings.* The choice was entirely my own, and I decided to consult Shklovsky for two reasons: 1) I intended to devote myself not only to writing but also to literary theory. 2) In that period, my ideas corresponded with Shklovsky's, Tynyanov's, and Eikhenbaum's, much more than they did with other writers'.

**Investigator:** All three ringleaders of formalism . . . But Soviet criticism condemned formalism long ago as an enemy of the real world and socialist realism in literature . . . It is commonly known that Shklovsky has a hostile stance towards the world around him and it is also commonly known that he has engaged in anti-Soviet activities for some time. It is also commonly known that after a certain point your relationship with Shklovsky had the same anti-Soviet character. I advise you to testify honestly and openly about this matter during your next interrogation . . .

December 29, 1978; 29 degrees below zero. "Better to die of fear than of cold," I decided, leaving the hotel and heading for the Mayakovskaya metro station (which was thirty-three meters underground). This novelty—usually I walked back and forth in front of the hotel for ten minutes or so waiting for a taxi—alarmed my escorts. For a week, eight young men in fake leather jackets (lined, I assume, but how on earth did their legs, their behinds, not freeze?) had been following me in a pair of mouse-colored Moskviches. Every morning they followed me all the way to the courtyard in front of the Writers' House, and when I left the Shklovskys' in the afternoon or evening, I would find them just where I had left them. Then they followed me back to the "Pekin," (a KGB-cooperative hotel, right in the center of town on the corner of Sadovaya and Gorky). I had learned the pointlessness of "whys" by then, and as an official guest of the Union of Soviet Writers, complete with a contract from the VAAP (All-Union Copyright Agency, Literary Branch of State Security) and the approval of Counselor Veselitsky, I felt almost at ease. He had come to pick me up at the airport, almost solemn, and after a courteous squeeze he led me to "Table no. 1" at customs—the one reserved for diplomats and distinguished guests, where nobody got searched. Furthermore, meteorological conditions kept me from going out at night, and when I called friends I certainly wasn't talking about Sakharov or Bukovsky. The only thing that worried me was that these bloodhounds carried out their task in such a brazenly obvious way, making no attempt whatsoever to keep a low profile—

when I took a taxi they didn't even follow at a safe distance. One day, after checking the rearview mirror several times, the elderly driver burst out: "Oh fuh . . . ! Your syphilitic mother should have aborted you! Antichrists! Satan's hemorrhoids! Sacks of stinking vomit . . . Let's lose 'em." "No, please." Why complicate my life even more?

The Petenky (that's what I called the four in the Moskvich with license plate 79-54) returned happily to their toasty car, which they always kept running, while the Vovochky (the ones with plate number 59-60) trailed me on foot, much less happily, to the metro. I was able to get a look at them: light eyes, high cheekbones, hard Slavic features, blank and icy stares.

It was noon when Shklovsky threw me out: "Get out of here!" Upset, my tears hardening into crystals on my cheeks, I headed straight for the Aeroport metro stop. Once again, my escort split up—this time it was the Petenky's turn to follow me through underground Moscow. They must not have enjoyed the ride on the crowded train; at the Mayakovskaya stop they escorted me off with a shove. As I fell to the ground, I felt—through several layers of wool and a fur coat—a colossal kick on my right side. I was on the ground when I came to, surrounded by concerned bystanders. Two police officers arrived. "What's going on here? Is she drunk?" "She's not," one lady answered, "but those four *huligany* who knocked her down certainly were, I saw them with my own eyes, they're right over there." I lifted my head a little: the Petenky were standing a few meters from our huddle and for the first time their lips stretched into little smiles. I saw the *militsionery's* boots march over to the would-be thugs and come back in less than a minute: the KGB badge terrorizes even the police. One of them took me back to my hotel. An hour later, a doctor came. A broken rib, most likely. "Apply this ointment and bandage your chest tightly." "With what?" "It's up to you; if you prefer, you can go to the trauma ward, but I'd advise against it—with this cold, you'd have to wait for hours at the emergency room. Most importantly, be careful not to laugh." That was the last thing I felt like doing. I cut up one of my pajamas and wrapped the strips around my chest, howling with pain. Shklovsky called: ". . . My God, I made you cry, forgive this crabby old man. I'll expect you tomorrow."

I asked if I could dine in my room: "We don't do that here." I went down to the restaurant and for a nominal fee of fifty rubles they put me at a small table off to the side;

as usual, I ordered soup and Peking chicken, and for once, a double vodka (200 grams). I went back up to my room, lay down for about half an hour, and went back down just in time to sip the broth with bits of Chinese mushrooms floating among the traditional *pelmeni*. The orchestra was playing "Midnight in Moscow." Back in my room, I rested again, and then went back for the second course. Seeing me heading for the elevator again, the guard for that floor asked me: "Is there something wrong? Up and down, up and down..." "Is that not allowed?" "No, but it makes our job difficult." He didn't specify which.

December 30. 34° below zero. Serafima Gustavovna draped a blanket over her husband's body like a peplos, brought in an electric heater, and then got into bed, in her clothes, under two tartan blankets. She was snoring by the time Viktor Borisovich finished his long, sad tale. As I was softly saying good-bye and asking about the plan for the following day, Shklovsky interrupted me: "Sereno-chka, tomorrow is New Year's Eve, I want to give Sima a present. With the royalties from my translations abroad I've been able to stash away a little money, that is, *tser-tifikaty*, but I've never set foot in a Beryozka. My Sima neither. And she dreams of having a *dublyonka*. They sell them at the Beryozka by the Novodevichy Monastery, she found out. Would you be willing to take her?" "Now???" "No, she's tired, poor thing. Tomorrow. Since it's a holiday the store will be almost empty, you'll be able to take your time." "And how will we get there and back?" He struggled to free his right arm from under the blanket, grabbed an address book and handed it to me. "You look, please, I don't want to get my other glasses. Under V: Veselitsky, Afanasy Veselitsky, Writers' Union." Stunned, I replied: "Veselitsky? Do you know him, what kind of guy he is, how much he drinks?" "Of course. No less than the Central Committee put him in that position; he could drink even a whole distillery of vodka and no one would be able to move him from that chair. But he's useful, and he can get us a car from the Union—am I or am I not a living icon?" He cleared his throat, summoned his threatening Dantonesque tone, and dialed the number. "Shklovsky here . . . Afanasy Aleksandrovich, tomorrow I need a . . ." After he hung up, he told me that a car would come pick us up at two on the dot.

Who'd have ever thought—even the eighty-something Serafima Gustavovna had been seduced by the *dubly-onka*. The original sin came from Lelouch and the film

*A Man and a Woman*: the sheepskin overcoat Anouk Ai-mée wore became the dream of Soviet women for years (though the men's version was also much sought-after), a symbol of western chic, privilege, affluence.

"What a horrible day you picked!" Afanasy said to me as he helped Serafima Gustavovna into the car. "I had to make a hundred telephone calls to find a driver . . ." It was a miracle that he'd found one, he added, so he would take advantage and run a few errands; he would be back to pick us up at five sharp.

During the trip to the Novodevichy Monastery (an ancient, splendid convent, where Chekhov and Gogol are buried: the ghost of the latter no doubt wandered around the "hard currency" store nearby to rob the fortunate clients of their warm, elegant overcoats), I turned two or three times to look out the back window. The Petenky and Vovochky were still there. Afanasy, who must have downed at least one vodka already, didn't notice a thing.

Around the Beryozka the snow had been cleared to make paths for vehicle access. Cars were scarce, as were customers, and Serafima Gustavovna had at least three salesgirls at her disposal to try on the *dublyonki* for sale. She couldn't find one like she wanted—with a hood and not too dark, "otherwise it would age me." We moved on to the hats, without much luck. As a gesture to the saleswomen, who had been unusually kind, I bought a kind of fur turban: it made me look vaguely like Josephine Baker, but it paid off in warmth when we left the store at five—but no Afanasy and no car. We waited between the two doors, where we could feel some of the heat from inside, but after five minutes poor Serafima Gustavovna could hardly stand up. "That's what I get for trying to look stylish at my age," she mumbled, trembling. I took her back inside and asked for a chair. After we'd lost an hour and all hope (Afanasy's errands must have been of the alcoholic variety, perhaps the driver had taken him to the hospital—if he wasn't drunk himself!), I realized that I absolutely had to catch a taxi, hail down a car: planting my feet firmly in the hard snow I went down the path to the street and stood there, waving my right hand persistently. I couldn't stand it for long, and after a few minutes I went back inside the Beryozka. Every time I came out, from the parallel paths, the Petenky and Vovochky put their cars into first and moved forward toward the street, only to reverse when I went back into the shop, completely frozen. I asked if I could call the Writers' Union.

Nobody picked up, of course. I resumed the quest: it was pitch dark, no cars except for my escorts'. Consumed with a desperate rage, I suddenly turned toward the Petenky on my left and practiced in my head what I was going to say: "At least let an old woman in your car to get warm, she could catch pneumonia. That would be a way to serve the State too!" Seeing me approach, the Petenky at the wheel of the 54-69 moved forward. In all honesty, I don't know how it happened—they slid on the ice, or he was caught off guard, or he wanted to punish me for the unexpected insubordination, or the path was too narrow . . . When the Moskvich and I were side by side, the Petenky swerved toward me, forcing me to lunge onto a heap of snow so as not to be hit head on. By then the snow had become solid hard ice, rocklike . . .

I limped back to the shop. I slipped, I said. One of the salesgirls felt bad for us: if we waited until closing, her husband, a taxi driver, would help us when he came to get her. I called Shklovsky to tell him we would be late.

I managed to get Serafima Gustavovna back home and return to my hotel. No doctors at that hour, that night. After less than thirty minutes (they were even nice at the switchboard on New Year's Eve), I got through to an Italian journalist friend who was in town. Surprised, he asked me how much I had drunk (if I'd been calling from Italy, it would have been well after midnight); he listened when I asked him for help, using "butterfly code": **I**-fi **am**-fam **in**-fin **big**-fig **trou**-fruh **ble**-full, etc. The thought of a decoder trying to understand the secret language of my childhood made me smile, despite my aches and my hunger.

The next morning my room was host to a real parade. First, the doctor. "Well, what have you been doing, you're one big bruise. You drink too much. Stay in bed for at least two days and put some ice on your hip and thigh." Then it was the man in the gray coat's turn: "Technical assistance. I have to fix the phone." "But it works just fine!" "That was the order. If you could please leave the room for a moment." I revealed what bandages I could. "Don't worry, I won't look." But I did: he casually unscrewed the receiver, inspected it, took something out, put something else in . . . The butterfly language must have made some ears burn. Third, my Italian friend arrived. "Let's go to the foreigners' hospital," he limited himself to saying, and on the way ("you can talk, the car is safe") he listened to my story. He had been in Russia for ten years and had never heard of anything like that happening . . . And to a foreigner . . . "Is your room clean?" "Spotless." "Then be careful, something's up. As soon as you get back to your hotel, don't leave your room. They could slip drugs into one of your books, in a drawer. And leave as soon as you can." He had a friend at Alitalia who could change my ticket. After the doctor's visit (just two cracked ribs and some contusions on my left leg), he took me back to the Pekin and made sure that nobody had paid me a visit while I was out.

Shklovsky called. Afanasy had gone over to apologize; the car had run out of fuel and he'd gotten stuck outside of town. "You can imagine—he smelled like Tsar Nicholas' wine cellar. But he didn't get off scot free, I whacked him with my cane . . ." He thanked me for getting Sima home safe and sound and ordered me not to come see him for at least two days, so I could rest and get better.

I grabbed my brightest, shiniest sweater, went out, locked the door, and with clear tape I attached two hairs, crossed, over the keyhole (which I'd seen in a spy film). A bribed waitress brought me provisions for two days. On January 3, after pulling out two more of my hairs, I went back to Shklovsky's for what would be, I announced, our last conversation: I had to go back to Italy—serious family problems—but I had gathered enough material . . . The pained look of those two was touching. When his wife left the room to prepare the tea, Viktor Borisovich said to me: "You're terrified, Serenochka, I know that look in your eyes very well. I have for fifty years. You don't have to tell me anything, but for the love of God, leave, go back to Italy. Nadezhda Mandelstam once said that we were living in a torture chamber. Today I call it an operating room. Every day they give us the anesthetic of fear, an ether that paralyzes the soul."

The morning of January 4, Afanasy drove me to the airport. Queasy again, with a few more bandages than before, I remained silent the whole ride. Once we reached Table no. 1 he pulled out his own identification and mine. The Petenky and Vovochky pounced on us like starved vultures. Afanasy's eyes bulged, the employee at Table 1 paled. A Petenka gestured for me to open my suitcase, then to follow him to a room where I was met by a woman in uniform. Once the door was closed, the policewoman (?) said to me politely: "Please, if you're hiding something—jewelry, drugs, papers—tell me, I don't want to have to search you." I emptied my pockets and my purse. That didn't convince her. "Since you don't want to cooperate, please remove your clothes." Later, the same woman took me to passport check and from there to the exit; my bags, she explained, would be returned to me on the plane.

I was alone on the bus and on the ramp. On the plane I was greeted by the sarcastic applause of the other passengers, who had been waiting over four hours on the runway. The flight attendant quickly ushered me to first class—empty, or emptied, for the occasion.

Back home, I found a piece of paper in my suitcase with a pencil sketch of my hair dryer and four pages on which someone had diligently copied the names up to "B" from my address book, including their phone numbers and addresses. Careless, the KGB! And what a disappointment: everything by hand, no photocopies . . . Even the legendary KGB, I now realized, suffered the inexorable constraints of the Soviet *defitsit*.


2003. Vladimir Voynovich's "Dossier n. 34840" is made public:

" . . . After that nobody touched me again, physically, but there were assaults on those who came to see me, even on those who didn't. The Italian Slavicist Serena Vitali [sic] was the guest of my neighbor Viktor Shklovsky, and when she left and got on a trolleybus, she was hit in the head with something heavy wrapped in a newspaper. During the attack they said to her: "If you see Voynovich one more time, we'll finish you off.'"

Was Voynovich—ever since *Private Chonkin*, in open battle with the regime—the real reason for my little (you know, word travels, information gets exaggerated . . .) mishap? Out of respect for the much more vicious attacks others went through, due to my now firm disbelief in a logic to violence, out of laziness, ultimately, I never asked to see my file when the Lubyanka opened its archives. The Petenky and Vovochky? I can see them now, bodyguards for some powerful nouveau riche. Or perhaps they have gotten rich themselves and they ride around in black six-door limousines. Or they scrape by with the modest pension afforded even the most idiotic KGBists, no longer of use to anybody . . .

SERENA VITALE, 2010

Shklovsky: Witness to an Era

## December 23

ON THE INFINITY OF THE NOVEL. ART HAS NEITHER BE-
GINNING, MIDDLE, NOR END. EPILOGUES ARE CLOYING
LEFTOVERS. ART DEALS ALWAYS AND ONLY WITH LIFE.

*My first question, Viktor Borisovich, is not so much about
what you've written as it is about what you haven't written.
Why is it that in these last two decades, which have seen
such a massive revival of your activity as a literary critic
and historian, you've never—or certainly very rarely—
commented on the themes or problems of contemporary
Soviet literature?*

I'm guilty, I admit. I don't work much on contemporary
literature. To tell the truth, I haven't been crazy about
what I have read. But, I repeat, the fault is mine. I hope
to take on this task, at least in part, to remedy this lack,

in my next book, which will have a great title, taken from Tolstoy: *Energy of Delusion*. The fact is that new, contemporary material will always pile up and then slip away, whereas the classics don't go anywhere, they endure. Please, you be the interpreter of my excuses for the Italian public, but this time too I'm going to limit myself to talking about literary material that's generally known, that has become the patrimony of all humankind. One author who I worked a lot on, for example, is Boccaccio. My book also came out in Italian. What did I want to say, and what do I still stand by today? Essentially this: art derives from the fact that man is marked by contradictions. And in art these contradictions can be resolved more or less favorably, but completely favorably—that's impossible. You know why I can't bear to read Dante's *Paradiso*? Because I believe that, normally, novels cannot be finished. Look at the beginning of Aristotle's *Poetics*: "A whole is that which has a beginning, a middle, and an end." With that, of course, I agree. But let's try to apply this concept to art. Let's take our literature, Russian literature. It struggles to comprehend the world, and the world has no end. In *War and Peace*, Pierre's nephew Nikolenka has a dream. Right at the end of the novel. He dreams of him and Pierre at the head of an enormous army made of white lines fluttering in the air like spiderwebs. Glory is before them, the same as those threads. At a certain point, the threads begin to go slack, to tangle. And Nikolenka and Pierre come upon Uncle Nikolai Ilyich Rostov standing there in a menacing pose and saying: "I loved you, but Arakcheev has given me orders, and I'll kill the first one who moves forward." What does the boy see? He sees the future, his own future. In the dream the boy is already the man of Dostoyevsky's era, of the Petrashevsky Circle. Art always projects itself into the future. Let's take, finally, the end of *Crime and Punishment*: Raskolnikov is in the penal colony, he doesn't like the prisoners who, in turn, are hostile to him, but a change starts to take place in him and his transformation is itself a potential novel. Exactly analogous to that is the end of *Resurrection*: the story of Nekhlyudov's transformation also contains another novel. But that novel was not written. That's why I say that there are no novels with an ending. A novel can come to an end, but it has no ending. Thackeray said that every time he wrote a novel he wished that the valet who shined his shoes would take care of the ending for him. And Tolstoy writes: "My God! Who'll finish the novel now!" And he says that because finishing his novel would mean knowing the future, and we don't know the future. *Eugene Onegin* isn't finished. Friends tried to convince Pushkin to finish it, but he didn't. And why? Pushkin is going through the post-Decembrist repression. As he's writing *Onegin* many of his friends are already dead, or far away, in exile. Pushkin can only send them a few coded messages. He can write, citing the epigraph to "The Fountain of Bakhchisarai":

> But those to whom, as friends and brothers,
> My first stanzas I once read—
> 'Some are no more, and distant . . . others.'
> As Sadi long before us said.
> Without them my Onegin's finished.

*But in the case of* Onegin *it was also a kind of self-censorship . . .*

Of course. In fact, what would Onegin's fate have been? In all likelihood he would have become a Decembrist. Everyone knows that some of Pushkin's verses are in code, and there's a clear allusion to Decembrism, that "storm" which Tolstoy said had spread over Russia like a magnet, attracting all the iron from the heaps of trash. In his notebooks, Pushkin drew the hanging of the Decembrists, and next to the drawing he wrote: "I could have. . ." It was only chance that kept him out of the revolt. When the emperor asked him, "Where would you have been?" Pushkin, as an intelligent, courageous man, replied: "On the square." And Onegin would have been there too. And Pushkin drew all this. He drew the Peter and Paul Fortress, with Onegin and Pushkin looking out at the Peter and Paul Fortress.

*And yet Tatiana's refusal in some way constitutes the "ending" of the novel.*

Tatiana, love—these are marginal things. Pushkin couldn't finish *Onegin*. It got swept up in history. History can extend the novel just as it can obstruct it. Otherwise it would be absolutely impossible to understand, for example, why the masterpieces of Homer have no ending. There was no censorship, there wasn't even a written text, there was nothing to erase. At the end of *The Iliad* and *The Odyssey* there's nothing but talk of the future. In general,

I think, talking about a beginning, middle, and end has nothing to do with art. We can also listen to a writer much closer to us than Homer, the great Chekhov, who says: when you begin writing, when the work is ready, tear out the first two or even five pages and never read them again. He also says: every time, the hero dies or leaves in the end. But that isn't a true ending. Tolstoy writes that he can't finish his novels. Why? Because if the character dies, it's interesting to see how the others survive him, but then the attention would shift to these others. If he leaves, it's the same thing. And if he marries, that's where the real story begins, the real conflict. Tolstoy wrote fourteen beginnings for *War and Peace*. But the novel has no end, because the fact that Natasha has grown old, that she's no longer so alluring, the fact that Pierre will most likely be deported and she will most likely follow him, all this isn't an end—the true ending is Russia, the unknown future of Russia.

*So on the one hand, the impossibility of knowing the future makes it so that a writer can't "finish" his novels; on the other, it seems like the great novels you've been talking about contain some sort of prophecy of the future.*

The fact is that the writer "predicts" the future, but doesn't know what his role in that future will be. He struggles with the future, he's afraid for himself . . . You see, he has to be very naïve to delude himself into believing he can bring something to a conclusion. And I myself, with all the love I have for novels, I prefer to doze off before the denouement. About epilogues—Thackeray wrote that they're like the lump of sugar left at the bottom of the cup. That's it—the conclusion, in the novel, is a cloying additive. It only appears to conclude things. For example, how do the great books end, the great tragedies of Dickens? Abruptly and by chance the man rediscovers his place in society and in life. The illegitimate son is acknowledged by the father, or the hero marries, or receives his inheritance, or leaves for Australia, but it's just a convention. And the fact that Othello kills Desdemona, yes, of course, that's the end: it's Desdemona's death, it'll be Othello's death. But that isn't the resolution to the theme of fidelity and love.

*So for you, the novel—or poem, or play—is a place where the contradictions of life cannot be resolved.*

That's precisely it, they can't be. When I read Kafka, who parodies the irresolvability of the contradictions of life . . .

*In what sense does he parody it?*

He exaggerates it.

*You like Kafka, no?*

I love Kafka. I love Remizov. I love this writer that almost nobody knows, Olga Forsh, who wrote novels and stories based precisely on this impossibility of a final denouement. But that's another subject. For example, take *The Cherry Orchard*. All classic novels have the figure of the devoted servant. We Russians knew him from the works of Walter Scott, Pushkin's, and Tolstoy's too, though to a lesser extent. But Chekhov ends his play in a very odd way. The serf Firs, alone in the house, says: "They've forgotten me." What does that mean? He too will get out. He won't be locked in forever. But one of the threads of that type of comedy has been forgotten. The master has one story, the servants another. The fact that in Chekhov the play doesn't end with Lopakhin's marriage, in other words, with a happy ending, is in itself surprising, compared to classic stories. But even more surprising is that Chekhov concludes with a man locked in, and he emphasizes it, and how—the sound of a string breaking, silence, then the sound of the axes cutting down the trees in the orchard . . . When an era ends, time sighs, and forms age. You see, we Russians, and you Italians too, we've all lived through an unfinished novel. And I don't know how a novel could end, just as I don't know what will happen in the world, what the future of Europe will be. The only thing I know is that one must always invent new endings.

*Insofar as the novel has no end, does it therefore reject the idea of death?*

Art always and only deals with life. What do we do in art? We resuscitate life. Man is so busy with life that he forgets to live it. He always says: tomorrow, tomorrow. And that's the real death. So what is art's great achievement? Life. A life that can be seen, felt, lived tangibly, a life that one can renounce, just as Othello does, forsaking his dreams of love and glory.

# December 24

THE MEMORIES BEGIN. CHILDHOOD IN PETERSBURG. HOW
TO EAT BLINTZES. DIGRESSION ON THE DRAWBACKS OF
HAVING A SECRETARY. SHKLOVSKY MEETING MAYAKOVSKY,
HE DOESN'T REMEMBER EXACTLY WHEN; THE BEGINNING
OF THEIR FRIENDSHIP. THE FUTURIST EVENINGS—THE
TECHNIQUE OF SCANDAL. BAUDOUIN DE COURTENAY. PO-
ETS SHOULDN'T BE ALLOWED TO DIVORCE. SEMINARIANS
AND CARPENTERS DUKING IT OUT ON THE ICE.

*Today, Viktor Borisovich, I would like you to say something
about yourself. Let's try to follow the timeline of your literary life. What were, and what was the nature of, your first
encounters with literature?*

The first writer I knew is someone that nobody remem-
bers today. To tell the truth, nobody knew him before ei-

ther. His name was Shakhparnians. He wrote lyrics for romances and had a good library. He only published in a provincial newspaper, but he was very serious about himself and about poetry—he lived for poetry. Besides that, he wrote handbooks for students: how to write essays that will please teachers. Here's what happened to this man: one day, after the revolution, I saw a beggar on the street. He approached me and asked me for money. Suddenly, I recognized him. Terribly startled, he said: "Listen, come to my house. I'm not so bad off. I married a woman who works in a pub. She loves my poems, she knows them all by heart. But she won't let me sell my library, which I'd rather sell so I can buy new books. Now you can get wonderful books for next to nothing."

*It's curious that you bring up this writer who left nothing behind . . .*

When I met him I was twelve years old. This Shakhparnians, an Armenian, was a minor poet, insignificant, but he's still the first poet I ever met. He knew my parents. Once Maykov wrote my father a letter, a letter about a student at my father's school. The minor Armenian poet and that letter were perhaps, during my childhood, my only "live" encounters with poetry. What am I trying to say with this? That we, my family and I, lived a thousand kilometers away from poetry, a thousand kilometers away and there were no telegrams, no news. On the other hand . . . Gorky, at the beginning of the revolution, defined the pre-revolutionary period in poetry and art as "shameful." But he was wrong. Why? In that period Tolstoy was waning, Chekhov was writing, Fet was winding down, Blok was getting started. In music, Shostakovich, Scriabin were starting out. From the window of your own house, even if the window is very high up, it's hard to recognize your own time. Usually we see our era as a series of close-ups. The most important man is always the one you're talking to now. And the most important time is the one you're living in. The person who said that, at the very end of his life, was none other than Lev Nikolaevich Tolstoy.

*You spent the first part of your life in Petersburg. How do you remember this "fateful" city of Russian literature?*

The Petersburg of my childhood? Picture a city where the snow is clean, white, exceptionally white. There's no sound of cars. The streetlamps are fuelled by oil; only downtown are they electric, and they cast a bluish light. A city filled with pedestrians, lots of whom wear long aprons that go past their knees: clerks in the various shops. Carriages pass by. The coaches in the square have very small horses, they're country horses that the peasants, so as not to let their animals eat for free, send to the city for hire. And the sleighs. Small. They can barely fit two people. But in spring, when the roads are in bad shape from the thaw, the *veiki* come, the Finnish coachmen. They come with these splendid colts, and the carriages have bells and curtains made of different colored strips of cloth. This is during Carnival. And during this time we eat blintzes. We eat tons of them, everybody makes them, and you have to make them, otherwise you have to explain why not to your neighbors. Delicious blintzes, made with buckwheat. We would eat them, I remember, with *snedki*. Snedki are tiny fish that were caught in the lake in Gdov, by Petersburg. The lake was overpopulated and the fish were tiny, smaller than a pinky finger. There was an enormous amount of them and they were sold for next to nothing, four kopeks a *funt*. All this was before the Revolution. At that time, in general, food was inexpensive. For example, in the taverns—there were many, then—for five kopeks you could get borscht with meat and bread, the bread was on the house, and when someone went back once or twice to the same place, they would bow and call him by name and patronym . . . Yes, Petersburg is a splendid city . . . Mendeleev, Blok, Esenin, Pushkin, Lenin, Khlebnikov, Mayakovsky . . . It was a unique city, completely different from Moscow. Moscow was wealthier. There was a strong merchant class. But don't think of just Ostrovsky's merchants. There was also a class of educated, enlightened merchants, some were true patrons of the arts. In general, pre-revolutionary Russian culture was a great culture, in its own way incomparable. Anyway, the merchant class characterized Moscow, it was more a Moscow phenomenon than a Petersburg one. Belinsky once wrote, about Moscow and Petersburg, that Moscow does nothing, Petersburg creates nothing . . . What did he mean? Yes, sure, bureaucrats, they're the ones who create nothing. Petersburg, though, was a city with a certain life, a certain culture. And it should also be said that this city full of uniforms, this snooty city, the capital, with its distinguished places of presence and absence, as we used to say—this city paid hardly any attention to power. In fact, it disliked it out-right. Everybody did . . .

*In your memoirs you have often mentioned a fairly diffi-cult, torturous scholastic career. Why is that?*

I attended a school where I was constantly suspended, but still to this day I'm convinced that they weren't right to suspend me. The fact is that I had horrible handwrit-ing, I still do. Recently I sent a letter to a writer. He didn't respond for a long time, I took offense, then I found out from his secretary that he didn't reply because he hadn't understood a single word of my letter. So, as I said, I had terrible handwriting . . . But I'm still offended by that writer. I can't remember anyone—not even Gorky him-self, early on, not to mention Mayakovsky, or Blok—I don't remember any of them ever having secretaries. These new forms of social interaction, in my opinion, are negative. What goes through a secretary is already fil-tered, secondhand, whereas if someone comes to see you because he wants to talk . . . Gorky said he considered himself a doorman, a custodian. "Someone knocks on the door, I let him in, and in comes a new person with a new, completely new voice. I tell him: sit down, make yourself comfortable . . ." This sense of complete interest in man . . . I advise all writers, on every continent, to keep this wonderful habit . . .

*How did you begin your career as a writer?*

I was about seventeen. I wrote a bad prose piece that got published in a bad journal, *Vesna* [Spring].

*Bad perhaps, but somehow "historic" for the Russian avant-garde. Isn't that the same publication where Khlebnikov made his debut in 1908?*

Yes, it's true that all the good writers of the time wound up in that journal. It had a peculiar feature—they didn't pay for what they published. A displeasing feature, if you like, but interesting. A good thing. It was Shebuev's journal. He was famous in his own right. In 1905, in a humor magazine he published, there was a "portrait of the working class" with the caption: "His Majesty, the proletariat of all the Russias." They were able to get it in, barely, considering the times. If I'm not mistaken he was imprisoned in the Peter and Paul Fortress. Shebuev was the first publisher I knew. Then I went to see someone called Kulbin. He was a student of Pavlov's, a good student, and he had a very secure position, he was a doctor for the General Staff. He made a lot of money—he even had, at that time, a private motorboat. He loved art, he was a painter. I brought him two or three of my things. He had a Vladimir but of course it's not as if he wore the medal around the house. I remember one time, it was already during the war, he did me a secret favor: he granted leave to someone (that someone was my brother). After that, this Kulbin was called in by the military Chief of Staff. The chief asked him by what right had he granted leave to Mr. so-and-so. Kulbin: "Do you plan to write me up?" "Yes." "Officially?" "Officially." "Then have the courtesy to stand up and repeat what you just said, and I'll take a seat, since according to regulation no one is allowed to be seated in the presence of a Vladimir recipient without his permission. And furthermore, I have the right to inspect all the prisons and the bathrooms, men's and women's . . ." This man, who died three days after the February Revolution—and he died happy—it was this man who, after looking at some of my things, which in my opinion were very weak, he said to me: "You're a genius." I said: "Based on what evidence?" He answered: "Forget about evidence. First of all, don't give private lessons. I'll give you forty rubles a month for two years. That's ten percent of my earnings. And in exchange, you won't eat in the taverns, because you can't eat well there. Eat cheese and fresh onions. They have vitamins and they're filling too." And this Kulbin was one of the first Futurists. He was friends with Matyushin, with Guro.

*So, you were proclaimed a genius. And your studies, in the meantime?*

After the Shapovalenko Gymnasium (a bad gymnasium, that's why I was never suspended there) I enrolled in the Department of Philology at the University of Petersburg. Then I began spending time with Osip Brik, who lived on Zhukovskaya Street. I don't know what that street is called today, but it should be called Mayakovsky Street, because that's the street that comes up in his poems . . . Mayakovsky'll come back to life, go to Petersburg and ask: Where's Zhukovskaya Street? And they'll tell him: But that's been Mayakovsky Street for a million years, because that's where the poet shot himself, at his beloved's door. I remember that house, it was a tiny apartment. And Lili Brik was there. Now she's dead too, she died a few months ago. And Volodya Mayakovsky was there also. He wore a black tunic—before that, there was the notorious yellow shirt, the "poet's blouse." Why did he wear it? On the street where Volodya lived there were some typographers, mostly Socialist Democrats or Bolsheviks, but anyway they were politically engaged—they were very good, and since to print well you have to have your arms unencumbered, they wore tunics that went down to their knees. It was a work uniform, black sateen. Everyone said those typographers were excellent. My first book was printed by those same typographers, the "Italians" we called them, because they were open-minded.

*Do you remember when you first met Mayakovsky?*

Well, it was over sixty years ago. Inventing things is easy; it's remembering that's difficult. I've never kept a diary, and I regret it, because, as Pushkin said, the flow of the pen halts at the word that will be read with indifference, with coldness. Everyone who writes a diary always makes himself seem smarter than he is.

*Do you think that of Tolstoy's diaries as well?*

Yes, Tolstoy kept diaries, but as it turned out he had a secret one that he kept hidden in his boots. I think that his true diaries are his novels. Just as I think that the true diary of an era is poetry. It's a warmer, more precise, more poignant diary. But back to when I first met Mayakovsky. Someone asked me about that recently. And I gave three different versions. We may have met during one of the public events, the Futurist evenings, and Mayakovsky began doing these public appearances very early, in 1912 or '13. I remember one of those events, a Futurist evening, near the Kalashnikov Exchange. Baudouin de Courtenay hosted, or rather, participated in the performance. Baudouin was interested in Futurist art, especially in the phenomenon of trans-sense language. So was Kruchenykh, who himself created phenomena, let's call them, of trans-sense language. That is, he would invent words without meaning, like a baby's gibberish, revel in sounds as such. If I'm not mistaken, Mayakovsky was there that time too, Khlebnikov, and maybe Kamensky, a happy person, strong, always cheerful. I spoke too. The evening ended in a terrible scandal. We had no fear of scandals. Why not cause a scandal? I mastered the technique. Here it is: you win when you don't know how far you're willing to go. That's always the case—with scandals, brawls, fights, even in war. But if you know a priori when you're going to stop, then you've already lost. At the end of the evening, Baudouin left the room. I, just a simple student at the time, went after him and called after him. He stopped to chat and said that no matter what, the most important thing is democracy. That politics is what matters. "What you believe," he went on, "is misguided. But I must admit that you have your own window on the world. Eventually you'll see something from there. And you must preserve this gift." He said this to me personally. Baudouin de Courtenay was a scholar, a great linguist, a unique person, very proud, like a typical Pole. At one time, his calling cards said: "Baudouin de Courtenay, King of Jerusalem." He claimed to have documentation proving he had descended from the first kings of Jerusalem. His ancestors had lost all their possessions in the attempt to prove it. Anyway, Baudouin told me that the most important things are science and democracy. At the time, poetry was a diversion. Later, we came up against the very big, complex problems of reality. And not only were we foaming at the mouth, we were literally exhausted.

*And the other versions of how you met Mayakovsky?*

You see, in 1914, I was serving in the armored division. Someone told me that a certain Brik really wanted to meet me. I said: "But I know him well, Brik!" He was a soldier who was famous, among us, for having wrecked three cars in one go—he got in a car that was in gear, it lurched forward and hit another two. So I went to see Brik—not the one who had crashed the cars—and there I met Mayakovsky, whom I already knew, but not personally, just from seeing him on stage. Not our acquaintance, then, but certainly our friendship, began at the Briks'. Speaking of the Briks, there are some people, in Russia, who don't like them, who speak badly of them, people who don't like Mayakovsky. But Volodya, before he died, wrote in his note: "Lilichka, love me." I mean, we don't have the right to dispose of the hearts of our great poets. We don't have the right to separate Dante and Beatrice. Of course, actual institutions for divorce exist. But if we let poets divorce, we have to give up poetry. And Mayakovsky loved Lili for a long time, tenderly, and as I wrote in *Zoo*, poetry is always written on the road to love, and we have no right to separate love from poetry. Moreover, we don't know why birds sing. Today people think that a nightingale sings to say: Here I am, here I am, and let no other nightingales come and bother me. But perhaps it's singing for the female nightingales, or the baby ones. Or simply because it likes to sing. We don't know anything.

*You mentioned a "technique of scandal." It seems that Mayakovsky was an expert in scandal as well. What was the role of the audience in all this?*

One time, Mayakovsky performed at a women's institute. A good institute, the oldest in Russia, where women were able to earn diplomas. I wouldn't call it a flop. It was a mega-flop. A disaster. Mayakovsky declaimed a poem in which he says that the world will never be rid of schoolgirls. He loathed them. And in another poem he said that one day, the world, the nation, would turn to itself and say: My God, what have I done! And then he, Mayakovsky, would write something beautiful that everyone would understand. Another time, at another Futurist evening, Mayakovsky and I walked through the audience, and we didn't exactly have to elbow our way through, but it was definitely like a crowded square. On that occasion, Mayakovsky got shot down—how can I put it—not with blanks, but with real bullets. And yet they knew he was a talented poet. He was tall, handsome, with broad shoulders, a slender torso, a nice build, and an extraordinary voice . . . You asked me to talk about the past, you see. The past is multifaceted, complex. Let me tell you a story. In Petersburg, there was a huge bar of gold, I don't remember its exact weight, but it was very, very heavy. After some time they wondered where they should put it so that it didn't get stolen, and then they decided to just pretend it was copper. And that bar's still there, for over a hundred and fifty years, and no one has ever touched it, it has never occurred to anybody that it could be gold. And in art there's gold that isn't recognized as such, but it's still gold. Mayakovsky, Khlebnikov—they were gold. As well as other great poets of ours. As a child, Volodya went hungry. He was still very young when he entered the Communist party, and his mother was in the Socialist-Revolutionary party. One time, his mother, along with some others, organized an escape from a women's prison. She sewed clothing for the inmates so that they could change as soon as they were out. His mother had her political views, he had his. And so Volodya couldn't see his mother. Otherwise it would have complicated matters for both of them. He had no house in the city that was home. His mother was a beautiful woman, educated, from the Danilevsky family. Mayakovsky's own father came from a line of Cossacks. One of his ancestors, a high-ranking soldier in the army during Elizabeth's reign, had taken part in a revolt. Volodya's mother was a very modest woman. I went to see her a few years after Volodya's death. The house was in bad shape. Thoughtlessly, I said "Are things all right?" She understood what I meant and replied: "I can't put anything in here that Volodya never saw." It's hard for me to talk about these things. It's true, life can't be changed . . . There was also Khlebnikov, one of the Futurists. His father was a famous Orientalist. And the blind Burliuk. Hylaea. A tiny village on the steppe. The "stone women." One of these "stone women" was put on Khlebnikov's grave at the Aleksandr Nevsky cemetery . . .

The past emerges through details, particulars . . . In Petersburg, in pre-revolutionary Petersburg, there were brutal street fights. My grandfather, who was a gardener, lived by the Aleksandr Nevsky monastery, where the religious academy was. Across the way, there was the Okhta, the carpenters' neighborhood, with the church of St. Joseph, their patron saint. And there, on the ice, future carpenters would duke it out with future priests. These were the rules of the fight: naturally, you couldn't hide anything up your sleeve, that was strictly prohibited; if someone fell to the ground, you couldn't hit him under any circumstances; when one of them realized he couldn't fight anymore, he would take off his cap and set it on the ground, that was the sign that he had given up. But when someone was completely enraged and wanted to go all the way, he would throw his cap as far as he could and yell "To the death!" And that's what the group of Futurists was like: Khlebnikov, Mayakovsky, Burliuk, Kruchenykh, Kamensky . . .

*Viktor Borisovich, why this strange chain of associations from the Futurists to the brawls between seminarians and carpenters?*

Life isn't just long, but also a multitude, multifaceted. There were the Futurists, there were the Acmeists, and there was that seminary on the Neva, right at the river bend. And my grandfather would talk about these fights between young men, one against the other, with very strict rules . . . Life has many stories, like a building . . . We talk about the future, but at the same time we belong to the past. The bells of the monastery would ring, some studied to become priests, took exams, the other shore of the Neva was filling up with factories, and reality is this concurrence of different times . . .

# December 26

Young philologists meet and discuss literature at the University of Petersburg. The birth of formalism. Lev Jakubinsky. Yevgeni Polivanov. Poetry and time: "The Bronze Horseman." Poetry as the "deep joy of recognition." Shklovsky, says Blok, understands everything. Yury Tynyanov. Boris Eikhenbaum. How two ex-formalists argued the day Akhmatova died. Derzhavin's arrival spells the end of formalism. Man's destiny is the material of art. Which has to be shaken up once in a while, like a clock that stops ticking. On the futility of looking at flags.

*I propose, Viktor Borisovich, that we devote today's conversation to Opoyaz, the now legendary "Society for the Study of Poetic Language"—in other words, to formalism. I'd sug-*

*gest starting from the very beginning, from its inception.*

In that case, I need to go back to my university days. After gymnasium, I enrolled in the Department of Philology. The University of Petersburg was very old, for Russia, and it had famous, very well-regarded professors. One of the most respected in our department was Semyon Afanasyevich Vengerov. I remember he would give the students enrolled in his courses a kind of survey to fill out. We were to explain the reasons why we had chosen that discipline. I said, more or less: because I want to create and lead a new literary school. Several decades later, I had the chance to see that piece of paper again. Vengerov, who was very meticulous and filed everything, had kept it in his records. So, it was there, in the halls of the University of Petersburg, where everyone who would form Opoyaz met for the first time. During one of the first student meetings, in 1912, I believe it was, we were already arguing that Vengerov's work wasn't real literary work. That the encyclopedias with dates, the biographies of writers, were antiquated and useless, and anyway, had already been done. Now I'm going to make a confession: I never finished university. Why? Because I didn't have time, but also because I wanted to occupy myself *seriously* with literature. I studied rarely, I didn't take my exams. But at university, where I was able to meet people like Mandelstam, Gumilev, where there was an unbelievable rivalry between students in different disciplines, I met Lev Jakubinsky. He was a linguist, Baudouin de Courtenay's favorite student. We became very good friends. I remember we used to talk on the phone for hours. Our conversations about literary matters were just as endless. He studied the different functions of language, the functional differences between poetic and practical language, where the word becomes a signal, something like a traffic light, a colored flag. What is today defined as formalism began with these meetings among university students, meetings and discussions that were completely informal. Our group's first publication didn't appear until 1916. Many of us in Opoyaz were incredibly knowledgeable, dedicated linguists, people with academic backgrounds. There was also Yevgeni Polivanov. He only had one hand. He'd lost the other when he was young—to imitate a character from the *Brothers Karamazov*, he lay on the tracks as a train passed over. And the train severed his hand. We became great friends. He was a brilliant man. He studied with Baudouin as well. And he was also a remarkable Orientalist. He himself told me that one day, at the university, as he was listening to a lecture half-asleep, his head back, suddenly he felt something like a jolt to his brain—and, he said, that from that day on he began to understand languages. He knew twenty or so. On the street he could speak to the Gypsies in their tongue, he knew Korean, Chinese, Turkish, Japanese, and other, smaller languages. After the revolution he became a Communist, working for Comintern. He had a dream: to create a table of all the languages, like Mendeleev's. Unfortunately, this truly exceptional man learned to smoke opium in the Orient. After a certain point even that wasn't enough—he began eating it. And he told me that he found it absurd that people could spend their money on anything other than opium. He was an unbelievable character: one time, he went to the university to present, if I remember correctly, his doctoral thesis. He came to the classroom in a coat but no pants, just underwear. Everybody at the university knew him, so they let it slide. He began to speak; halfway through they told him he'd said enough, but he replied: "Dear colleagues and professors, please allow me to continue. I don't think you've understood anything yet." The presentation went well and he was awarded his degree.

*What was the reaction to the debut of the young—but, as it would seem, aggressive—theorists of formalism?*

Ah yes, we were aggressive, very. We certainly weren't gentle with our elders. But that was the era, it was indispensable. Anyway, the circle of old professors didn't make much of an effort to include us. Consequently, problems arose.

*And what was the relationship between Opoyaz and the Moscow linguistic circle?*

We had meetings with them, naturally. Jakobson often came here, he would stay in Petrograd. But they were two distinct groups. The fundamental difference between the Moscow group and the Petersburg group, I think, is that the Muscovite group, especially Jakobson, held that literature was a phenomenon of language, whereas we held that literature was one of the phenomena of artistic expression. But if literature is an exclusively linguistic phenomenon, it becomes impossible to understand how the translation of literary works is possible, or why the great upheavals in history could enter into literature without entering into language.

*In this sense, if I've understood you correctly, you consider Muscovite formalism closer to the approach of contemporary structuralism.*

That's probably true. In any case, their position is mistaken. It only allows you to study poetry, not prose. Anyway, I too was one of the first to make this mistake when, under Kruchenykh's influence, I wrote that poetry is an art exclusively of words, even if those words are nonsensical.

*Are you alluding to your essay "On Poetry and Trans-sense Language"?*

I am . . . But of course, that was pure insolence, I wanted to make a splash, shock people. As I've said, it was the era. Poetry, all poetry, even the most apparently "meaningless," is bound to its time and must be read in the context of that bind. Which is not merely a relationship of influence. And I don't really like that word. What's flowing into what? Neither time nor poetry are vessels into which something can be poured. Poetry, you see, lives in its own particular time. Poetry and real life, for example, age at different rates. Common time consists of years, decades, whereas poetry lives in centuries. The time of poetry is essentially the time of writing, of creation. Between the beginning and the end of a poem, there's an entire poetic destiny, and thinking that the first and second verses are contemporaries is an error. The time of poetry is the time of the creative act, the time of the making and changing of the poet's relationship with the world. It's the time of sensation, of the perception of reality.

*Yes, but then where can one find the traces of this bind, this intersection of real time and poetic time?*

Let's take an example from Pushkin, "The Bronze Horseman," which everybody knows. It begins with the verses: "There, by the billows desolate, / He stood, with mighty thoughts elate, / And gazed . . . " "He," of course, is Peter I, Peter the Great. And the poem ends with the flooding of Petersburg and the destruction of the house of Parasha, the woman loved by Yevgeny, a petty clerk, a civil servant. At the beginning of the poem Pushkin has Peter saying: "And here a city by our labor / Founded, shall gall our haughty neighbor." The city, Petersburg, will be founded, but this new city will also be the site of Parasha's ruin. In other words, the hero's story will turn out to be another man's fate. A hundred years after Peter decided to build the city, a hundred years later, a girl dies. How does Pushkin establish this continuity? In a poetic, nonlinear way. If at the beginning he writes: "The moss-grown miry banks with rare / Hovels were dotted here and there . . ." he's talking about the houses, the "shelter" of the "wretched Finns," at the end of the poem we'll again see a "frail hut," the small, rickety house of a petty bureaucrat. You see, this collision of epochs, of history, of destinies . . . without that, you can't understand the structure of a work.

*You have "confessed" to Kruchenykh's influence on one of your early critical works. This reaffirms, even if it's no longer necessary, the interrelatedness of the avant-garde and the formalist "school."*

I did, but about that essay—where I cite various examples of the glossolaliac language of mystical sectarians—I want to tell you a story. Once Polivanov told me that one of the examples of glossolalia I cited was actually from Old Tibetan. The text had been transmitted orally, and even though its meaning is no longer understood, it had become part of religious language. Originally, however, those words had a meaning and were fully comprehensible.

*In that essay, to argue for trans-sense language's right to a place in poetry, you also bring up a fascinating problem, about which much more could be said—namely, that sort of rhythmic "sound-picture" that precedes poetry and that, once poetry is formed into words and written down, determines our perception of it.*

You see, this is something that Mayakovsky has written about too. "I go about waving my hands and mumbling almost incoherently, slowing down so as not to disturb my mumbling, or mumbling quicker in order to keep time with my feet [ . . . ] Gradually, you begin to extract individual words from the roar. Some words bounce off never to return, others stick, are turned over and over and inside out dozens of times, until you feel that the word has fallen into place . . ." That is, even Mayakovsky says that the rhythm comes first, and then the composition, the "message," the key word that gives the entire poem its meaning. And in this process, the word tests the space around it, just as we grope for things around us in the dark.

*That image brings to mind the words of another great Russian poet, Mandelstam, who said that poetry is the "deep joy of recognition . . ."*

Yes, poetry is the "deep joy of recognition." That's it. The poet searches, gropes in the dark, and my dear contemporaries, so prolific in words, the structuralists, who filled the world with terminology . . . You see, they don't know this thing, this affliction of the presentiment of art and the joy of recognition. Only the great poets do. They know they're going to write. They don't know what will come out, whether it will be a boy or a girl, they only know that it will be poetry. Only the poet knows this tortuous search for the word, the physical joy of "recognition," and sometimes, also the anguish of defeat. Again, take Mandelstam: "I have forgotten the word I wanted to say. A blind swallow returns to the palace of shadows . . ." I knew Mandelstam, I remember him rushing down the stairs of the House of Arts declaiming these verses. You see, a poem is born from struggle. A rhythm, a word, like an echo, then a word with a different meaning, in the dark you only see individual, separate things, but then, little by little, your eyes adjust to the change in the light, they can see, and it's poetry.

*Viktor Borisovich, I understand that you too have written something in verse. I've seen some of your poems in the 1914 First Journal of Russian Futurists. Have you also experienced this "affliction of presentiment"?*

No, never, absolutely not. One might ask, therefore, how I can even talk about it. You know, one time Blok said to me—we were walking, it was night time, the Northern night, a white night, the stones were just barely pink, the Neva clear blue, and, God, since I've embarked on such a picturesque description, I might as well add that the sky had glints of scarlet. So, Blok and I were walking and talking. We talked for a long time that night. And at a certain point, he says to me: "Why is it that you understand everything?" Only that, it's terrible, but I don't remember at all what we were talking about. I still wonder today: what did I do to deserve such a compliment from this great poet? But I must say that I do understand a few things. Not everything, of course. But some things.

*Allow me to return the question of poetics for a moment. You've written a lot about Mayakovsky, and, among other things, about how he revolutionized poetry. But don't you believe that Mayakovsky's new poetry, and in general, much of modern Russian poetry, would have been unthinkable without Khlebnikov? Khlebnikov, who says "a line of verse is the movement, or dance, of a figure who enters at some doors and exits at others."*

Sure, I agree with you. And don't forget to put this line from Khlebnikov in the text of our conversation. The dance of a figure who enters at some doors and exits at others—there lies all the indeterminacy and richness of art. Man lives in the world, but first and foremost he lives in the world of words. And from the "displacements," from what seems discordant, from transgressions, often comes a new harmony. Khlebnikov talked about the child's marvelous transgression. Rhyme, but perhaps not just rhyme, all poetry, might predate the world, might already live on the child's lips as soon as he starts to babble, to realize that sounds can be put together.

*That brings to mind another question. What role did Andrei Bely's research on Russian prosody have in the emer-*

*gence of the formal method?*

Sure, Bely was a big influence. On all of us. Of course, not everything he wrote was correct. But first you have to read Bely, then you can criticize him. You should be afraid of the books you agree with, not the ones you disagree with. You should be afraid of the books you haven't read, not the ones you have. Khlebnikov, for example, knew Bely by heart. I mentioned Bely's errors. With metrics, Bely *draws* the rhythm, makes a diagram of the meter. But these are only the traces, the footsteps of poetry. It's a spatial graph. But in poetry, as I was saying, there's the time element. You also have to take into consideration the pace of a poem.

*Assuming all the responsibility for the long digression this time, I'd like to ask you to go back to your memories of the University of Petersburg, Vengerov's irreverent students . . .*

With us, there was Yury Tynyanov. He was a little younger than me. And he was a better student than me, he took all his exams . . . I cherish his books. In one he wrote the dedication: "If I hadn't met you, my life would have been spent in vain." Yet he had a great life. We're not the ones who invent ourselves, it's time that invents us. It invents us then it abuses us. Yury wrote poetry, beautiful verses in the style of Derzhavin, he loved Küchelbecker, the poetry of the Pushkin era. He had a deep understanding of poetry, he would talk about the "density" of verse. He said that the poetic word, because of a line's power of compression, became more "effective" than the prosaic word. Yury wrote that splendid book that is *Archaists and Innovators*. I remember I suggested he change the title, I mean, put a hyphen instead of the *and*. Because an innovator is always an archaist. For example, the taste for folk decoration played an enormous role during Manet's times. In other words, I'm referring to that return that's always there—in every moment of rupture and innovation—to the earliest sources, the primordial sources of the arts. And the Russian archaists . . . It was the War of 1812 and it turned out that the Karamzinists didn't have the right words for that reality. The archaists, Shishkov, had them. Russia came out of 1812 with new challenges, new tasks . . . And literature too came out changed. You can't understand Hermann and Raskolnikov without Napoleon. Just as you can't understand Balzac's heroes without him. But what was I talking about? "I have forgotten what I wanted to say. And a bodiless thought returns to the palace of shadows . . ." Yes, I was talking about my friends from Opoyaz. Boris Mikhailovich Eikhenbaum. I met him later, in 1916. He was a professor, a scholar. He had written in *Apollon*. He was four or five years older than me. He wrote an extremely interesting essay, "How Gogol's 'Overcoat' is Made." Interesting and important, focused on *skaz*, oral speech in Gogol. Gogol began with the word, of course, there's no arguing that. But beyond that, in Gogol, there's the revolt of the little guy. Even the name Akaky . . . According to legend, Akaky was a humble, meek friar; when he died and was buried, the starets who had oppressed him in life turned to him, during his eulogy, and said: "Are you resting, Akaky?" And Akaky, dead, responded: "Blessed are the poor in spirit, for theirs is the kingdom of heaven," that is, with the words from the Sermon on the Mount. In other words, there's humility and docility in the very name Akaky. But Gogol's Akaky Akakievich rebels at the end, he speaks with the language that only the coachmen in the square use to express themselves. And at a certain point he says, I couldn't care less if you're a general. It's the revolt of the poor. A rich man, a millionaire who read the story, said: "How can people not make a fuss about this book in which some lowly man goes around stealing furs?" Akaky Akakievich rebels in death. He's a ghost in revolt. Also, in many respects, Eikhenbaum's work was taken up by Vinogradov. And his title was a response to my "How *Don Quixote* Is Made."

*Now that you mention it, Viktor Borisovich, it would be interesting to find out what you think of that today: how is* Don Quixote *made?*

When I wrote about *Don Quixote* I wanted to show how much parody there was before parody. In Cervantes there are three degrees of parody. There's Boiardo, Ariosto, and many others. But then there's another problem. Why, how, to what end, did this story of parody of parody come about? You see, explaining how long literary schools last by saying, as I did at one time, that a literary school comes into being because the previous one has become tedious—this is how, at most, one could explain how trends change: why today people wear tight pants and tomorrow they wear baggy ones. But it can in no way explain, for example, Pushkin's rise and fall. And, in general, the great problems of humanity—how Akaky Akakievich should live, what Golyadkin has to do, what the "poor folk" have to do—these problems exist and we can't say yes, we want them, or no, we don't. They surround us, and when Pushkin said, "I'll shed tears over a work of imagination," you can be sure he wasn't crying over one of Lotman's books. He had other problems, other scores to settle, there were other conflicts in his work, even if Pushkinian, from the Pushkin era. And when Pushkin began the *Onegin*, he immediately wrote: "This is the beginning of a long poem which will, probably, never see completion." It was '25, before the revolt, and no one knew what would happen . . . Art always echoes with the screech of icebergs scraping against the ship, keeping it from moving forward . . .

*Viktor Borisovich, you've talked about the beginnings of Opoyaz, the "circle" of students that had formed around '12 at the University of Petersburg; could you tell us now something about the end of Opoyaz and, in general, about the final days of Russian formalism?*

Well, after the revolution, we (Tomashevsky, Zhirmunsky, Vinogradov, Tynyanov, and I) taught at the Zubov Institute.

The owner of the building that housed the institute was, of course, Count Zubov. And—want to know something?— that same count, right when Yudenich was approaching Petrograd, asked to enter the Party. Yudenich was at the gates, you can easily imagine how being a Communist at that time wasn't among the most advantageous of positions. But his request was not accepted. I'm telling you this to give you an example of how devoted and willing our intelligentsia was in those days. I can cite another example for you. There was a writer in Russia who I think is completely unknown abroad, a children's writer called Charskaya. For the number of books she wrote she was definitely the most important writer of children's books. Her characters were frequently pupils in girls' boarding schools. I remember my sister had several of her books. Charskaya was an actress at the Alexandrinsky Theater. A modest actress, she always played minor roles. Then she was "bought" by the publisher Vulf, which published everything she wrote— and it was a lot—providing her a monthly stipend equivalent to what a schoolteacher would get. After the revolution, her heroines had become daughters of Communist parents and they mopped the floors, they looked after the house. Charskaya also requested membership in the Party. She was not accepted. And her son, if memory serves me right, died in the civil war here. But I was talking about the Zubov Institute, or rather, the Institute of Art History. It was on Saint Isaac's Square. It was like a university, a newly founded university. There were many, many students. I remember that one of them was a fireman. It was a fantastic school. I liked working there. And I was very well liked. When the Institute closed down—I mean, it didn't exactly close, but, it transformed, let's say—there was a joke circulating among the students. A professor had been sent to direct the Institute, a member of the Academy of Sciences called Derzhavin. It was the collapse of formalism . . . And the students, parodying Derzhavin the poet's "Ode on the Death of Prince Meshchersky," the verse where he says, "Where once a feast was spread a coffin lies," would say, "Where once a feast was spread a coffin lies, and on that coffin sits Derzhavin" . . .

*So the scholars in Opoyaz held public lectures, took part in debates . . .*

Yes. All the time. Even at the Hall of Columns. One time, I remember, Bukharin was there, as a respondent. We often held conferences at the Tenishev Institute . . .

*And do you remember the last, or one of the last, of these lectures? Or when the Zubov Institute was "transformed"? You see, Viktor Borisovich, I'm trying to put the dates together to figure out the "effective" end of Opoyaz.*

I don't know, I don't recall. In the second half of the '20s, anyway, the formalist group, as such, no longer existed. As far as I'm concerned, the story went like this. Erenburg's magazine *Vesch* [The Thing] was published abroad. And in it I had an article in which I begged Jakobson to come back to Russia so we could create a big formalist school. But at the time I was having serious political troubles. For my part, I didn't think it was right, seeing as my case had been closed so calmly and magnanimously by Chairman Sverdlov. But then it was reopened. A long time later. It was no laughing matter, my head was at stake. So I fled. Later, back in the Soviet Union, I had more problems over a book, *Hamburg Account*. Have you read it? Well, they got really angry at me: What's the meaning of this Hamburg account, why tally up a score in some other city? And what kind of score is it supposed to be if no one is responsible for it? . . . You ask me about the end of formalism—you see, we found ourselves surrounded . . .

*Yet besides this "surrounding" from the outside, there were also some centrifugal tensions on the inside, theoretical disputes between various members of the group, so they say. I'm thinking, for example, of the dispute between Opoyaz and Zhirmunsky.*

Viktor Zhirmunsky was my friend. A very cultured person; he'd had a Heidelbergian-German education. He left Opoyaz very quickly. He wrote a great deal on verse, and some of his pages can sink they're so dense, impenetrable even. Let me tell you something: one day, the day when Anna Akhmatova died, on the shore of the Gulf of Finland there were two people arguing furiously. It was me and Viktor Zhirmunsky. We met there and he said to me: "I know you so well, I've learned so much from you, but you, admit it, you've never read my books." And I said: "Listen, if the question is whether I read them or not, yes, I read them. But say I really read them all the way, well, that I cannot." Then we walked for a while, and we talked about Opoyaz. He had a dacha in that area, he was a professor. He had some vodka in the cellar. I've never been a drinker. And Viktor Maksimovich probably didn't drink either. Yet we drank a whole bottle that day. And we didn't even get drunk, because we were too sad. Our disagreements, in general, were like the fights in Gogol—do you remember "The Story of How Ivan Ivanovich Quarreled with Ivan Nikiforovich"? I mean, they were fights over nothing. There was a bitter moment, however, when I published *Notes on the Prose of the Russian Classics*. In that book I rejected everything: father, mother, dog, cat. I'm at fault, I realize that. And even before that I committed another misdeed. I had written *Zoo, or Letters Not about Love*, and when I came back to Moscow, I made some changes to the book, i.e., I tried to lessen the erotic tension. Gorky got really mad at me. And Tikhonov told me: "After something has been written it belongs to literature, you can't touch it, it's not just yours anymore."

*And if today, at almost sixty-five years after its inception, you were to give an overall assessment of your experience with formalism?*

Opoyaz was able to cover fairly broad territory, it was recognized in the academic sphere, but it was never able to master that other domain to which it owes its existence and for which it creates literature. Words are never a tower, or rather, if they are, they're a watchtower, a tower from which you look out onto the world. In other words, art has always had its vicissitudes, it has always lived in blood. Art has a particular life, a life that doesn't run parallel to real life, but remains in eternal conflict with it. I never finished my work in Opoyaz, and in general, the theorists of Opoyaz were never able to fully answer this question: how social problematics, entering into the sphere of art, change their essence. Today, I believe that Dostoyevsky cannot be considered apart from the penal colony, the city of Piter, from Fourier, the year 1848, the destruction of Europe. Tolstoy can't be separated from the pre-revolutionary era, from the assassination of Alexander II (and note that, during those years, Tolstoy was writing about nonresistance). You can't read *War and Peace* outside of Russia, outside the nineteenth century, Decembrism, the destiny of man. Man's destiny too is the stuff of art.

*And do you think that if there hadn't been external pressures and if there had been the time and a way, Opoyaz, at least you in Opoyaz, would have naturally come to this "revision"?*

I'm certain of it. You see, I'm not suggesting—as some have said—the end of formalism, but overcoming it. After all, what did Opoyaz accomplish? It made the first, violent impact. An impact that *had* to be made, with all its extremes. Art, like a clock that's stopped ticking, has to be shaken up. We provided that jolt. We were attacked, the pressure was strong, very strong, but we planted many seeds. There were already some students, and they continued and concluded the work we began. It was difficult, but they did it.

*With this "overcoming," you don't refute—in fact, I'd say you reaffirm, if you prefer, "enstrangement" as the basis for artistic vision.*

The world exists, a world we struggle with, always and forever, just as Robinson Crusoe struggles with nature on a desert island. We struggle with the world, but we don't *see* it. Robinson sits at a table and draws up a ledger, makes a tally: what's good and what's evil. But art doesn't tally up, it doesn't *recognize*, it sees. To touch, feel, perceive, this is the strength of art, which looks at the things of existence with wonder. Art is continuous astonishment. Wonder gives rise to a new perception of the world, man feels the world, makes it his own. Because of art it's as if we take off our gloves, rub our eyes, and see reality for the first time, the truth of reality. We're not the ones who create words. Words already exist, in the lexicon. Even when we build a car we're not doing everything from scratch, it's as if we were building it out of old parts from other cars. As if we were giving the old cars new meaning. Art, poetry make use of words, of preexisting structures, but through their collision they overcome and revive them, giving them a palpable and practicable sense.

*And what do you think, today December 26, 1978, of what you wrote in one of your books from the '20s,* Knight's Move: *"[Art's] color has never reflected the color of the flag that flies over the city fortress"?*

I'll just say that there's no need to stand around staring at flags. Because sometimes something turns out to be revolutionary that we knew to be anti-revolutionary, and then it turns out to be anti-revolutionary . . . and so on. But, of course, that theory of mine was incorrect.

# December 27

KHLEBNIKOV, FILONOV, AND A PAINTING THAT REFUSES TO HANG ON THE WALL. MALEVICH'S SQUARE. FEBRUARY 1917. MEMORIES OF WAR. A STOMACH WOUND. A KISS FROM KORNILOV. RUSSIA AND ASIA. RUSSIA AND EUROPE. ESENIN IN VALENKI. MAYAKOVSKY HAS THE LAST WORD: THE PEOPLE KNOW HOW TO DRINK.

*You were able to meet all the great writers of your time. You've talked about some already, later you'll say more. But today, I'd like to shift our focus to the great artists. You've written about painting. Perhaps you could say something about a figure as unique and significant—yet at the same time unjustly forgotten or repressed—as Pavel Filonov.*

Sure, I knew Filonov. But we weren't close friends. We were very meticulous when it came to the demarcation of groups, you know. He was in a different circle than I was. His own, separate. Then there was Malevich and Tatlin's, there was Chagall's . . . For example, when Malevich was director of the Vitebsk Art Institute, he didn't like Chagall very much. Among other things, they were divided on their ideas of figurality: Chagall was for the human figure, even if represented in the most fantastical ways, in flight, etc. Malevich, on the other hand, believed in geometric abstraction. I was closer to Malevich's group. And Filonov had his own group, Khlebnikov's. To him, Khlebnikov was a true authority. Filonov had a particular religious faith. He was a sectarian. He was a truly great painter, a good poet, and completely possessed. He drew strange, ghostly human figures, a little like the ones in religious icons; he drew them as if they weren't from our own time, as if they came from the century that discovered poetry. Filonov had had an extremely hard life; his students helped him a great deal.

*What do you mean by "possessed"?*

Let me tell you a story. Once, at the Stray Dog, Khlebnikov read a poem with anti-Semitic content. Yes, that's how he was, Khlebnikov, he was just made that way, there's nothing to be shocked about, he could have even proposed out of the blue that they eat one of the members of the group. Mandelstam, who was in the audience, said he felt offended as a man and a Jew and challenged Khlebnikov to a duel. There were a lot of people there. Khlebnikov wouldn't retract his poem and he asked me to be his second. Filonov was to be the other second. And so, Khlebnikov and I went over to Filonov's. I don't know if, from the protocol point of view, that was the right way to go about things . . . I'd been in a duel once, but unfortunately, all I managed to hit were the papers my opponent was carrying in his coat pocket. So, as I was saying, Khlebnikov and I went over to Filonov's. At the time, he lived on Vasilyevsky Island. On Dunkin Lane. "Dunkin" from Dunya, a common, very popular name for women. That street was famous because that's where the prostitutes lived. And in fact, at the entrance to the street there was a patrol (this was just before the war) that wouldn't allow soldiers to pass. Anyway, we were able to get through. Khlebnikov told Filonov his story. Filonov—who no less than worshipped Khlebnikov—heard him out and then said, "Where did you get such a strange idea? It's not up to the standards of our decade!" And Khlebnikov shot back: "In your opinion, what are the standards of our time?" Filonov replies: "Look, I did a painting and I want it to stay on the wall by itself, without nails." Without skipping a beat or seeming surprised, Khlebnikov asks, intrigued: "And how did that go?" "For the time being, I've stopped eating." "And the painting?" "It keeps falling down. I spend the day looking at it, staring at it, talking to it, I say: you stupid wall, what else do you want from me? You want Heaven to come and take me? Hold up the painting!" Then Khlebnikov asked him, again: "So what do you think about our squabble?" Filonov says, "I'm a calm, reasonable man. I think you're both great poets. What you're doing isn't up to the standards of our time . . ."

*In other words, Filonov believed in miracles?*

He didn't just believe in them, he expected a miracle every day. He was fascinated with primitive Christianity. He was convinced that, if someone truly believed, it was possible to walk on water. He expected the wall to be able to understand the greatness of his painting. Just as Tatlin wanted to fly. And, mind you, Filonov wasn't just mad that the painting wouldn't stay up without nails—he was astonished. But this whole school of avant-garde painters who saw Khlebnikov as an indisputable authority, every single one of them recognized the inevitability of miracles. What they were looking for was their pattern. They had little in common with this world, they didn't need anything.

*This asceticism is also noticeable in Khlebnikov's "style."*

Oh, Khlebnikov . . . If men live in houses, he lived out the windows. If men live in the woods, he walked on branches. His nomadism is no legend. He could change his route, when traveling, to follow the one bird that hadn't been scared off by him. I remember one time, on the way to Persia, Khlebnikov stayed with an old acquaintance of mine, whose surname I can't remember now. He was a colonel, I remember, and in those parts there was still the old government. Khlebnikov stayed at his house. This guy, my acquaintance, at a certain point says to him, "I'm an old man, I'm forty-five years old, I really can't understand what you're doing." And Khlebnikov, who was a man without a party: "You know, Vladimir Ilyich Lenin is ten years older than you. And yet he understands. Why can't you?" I'm telling you all this to give you an idea of the time. We were all in our twenties before the revolution, we thought that life needed to be rebuilt from the ground up. There were projects, plans. Often our ideas were juvenile. We were interested in the problematics of space and time: we understood that time can move forward as well as backward, and that space is the fourth dimension. Those artists, those painters, they were men that the revolution didn't fully know how to read. Malevich's Suprematist *Square* provoked indignant, violent reactions. Artists were taken aback. But even now that everything has become a little simpler, now that so much time has passed, if I saw a painting of that sort I would be astonished. And Malevich was perfectly convinced, in good faith, that his painting was a revolutionary flag. I've been told that Malevich took part in the 1905 Revolution. And he firmly believed that that was the revolution which understood. But the revolution that understands, that one is always in the future.

*In 1905, you were clearly too young to understand what was going on. But what was your experience of the events of 1917 like?*

I saw only the February Revolution firsthand. I'll tell you my story, would you like me to? I was working in the army as an instructor at the drivers' school. It was a three- or four-story building, in Petersburg, across from the Mont de Piété. A few days before the February events the authorities took the carburetors out of our armored cars, but we had some parts stored away. And almost everyone in the garage was a Bolshevik. Our school was a very good one. I knew cars, I even wrote a book on them. So, when the February Revolution broke out, my students told me that we needed to repair our armored cars. We went to a little garage, near the French Church, we fixed them and went out with two cars equipped with machine guns. The Volinsky Regiment was the first to rebel, the first day. The night before someone got killed and the next morning the regiment mutinied. I remember the first days of March. The soldiers before us were happy. We went around in our cars, the population disarmed the police without encountering any resistance. The various battalions, the infantry, the artillery, they mutinied. There was no real center to the rebellion. The factory workers acted immediately, perhaps even before the army. They closed the Winter Palace. They put Muslim soldiers on guard because they don't drink alcohol. But no one attacked the Winter Palace: the tsar was in Gatchina. The mob took Rasputin's body and set it on fire. The people hated him.

*And your war stories? You were at the front, you were wounded . . .*

You know, war is a strange thing. What I can tell you is that you don't think about death.

What I actually remember feeling was great astonishment. Astonishment that everyone around you is falling and you're still standing, you haven't been hit . . . Yes, during the time we're talking about now I had already been in war, on the western front, which is Polish territory today. Back on the front, after February, I found myself back alongside Stanislavov and I saw the traces of the war that had passed, not long before, through those places. I was young then. The government wanted to continue the war. There were terrible losses, a shortage of weapons, our artillery was good but we had bad positions. At a certain point, I remember, they decided to attack. It was raining. The soldiers didn't know what to do. I encouraged them. And I was the first to go. I still remember that feeling today—of walking but not knowing why. And the unit followed me. I was almost over the German line and I threw two grenades, one to the right, one to the left. I was young, then. But the soldiers were right when they had yelled that they wouldn't move. They weren't the ones who had chosen that war. We were tired, poorly equipped. But that day, I went on the attack because in Petrograd I had said I would, and I felt responsible for my promise. My friends at the time, my literary companions, especially Mayakovsky, would never have done it. At some point I was shot. I fell. Later, at the field hospital, a young doctor, after looking at my wound, asked for my home address. I hadn't realized it was so serious. Anyway, I survived. And while I was in the hospital, I remember, Kornilov visited (around that time there was Kornilov's attempted coup, but his soldiers didn't follow him). He gave me a medal and tried to kiss me, but I blocked him. What for? I said, I don't like to kiss people, especially men, and even less so with a wound in my stomach. Babel laughed and laughed about this story with Kornilov. You see, Solzhenitsyn is a good writer, not always of course, and he's a good journalist, but in mentality and politics he's a Kornilovite. I returned to Petrograd. For a little while before leaving again for Persia. The people were for peace and against the Germans. Everyone was for land reform. The Bolshevik party was very strong, and the Socialist-Revolutionary party was huge. Volodya was a Bolshevik. Blok wrote that he voted for the SRs once during that period and that his doorman was very happy. The SRs were a revolutionary party and yet they were indecisive. They didn't know what to do. But immediate action was needed.

*Now that you mention Blok and the revolution—in one of his works, right after the revolution, the poem, "The Scythians," Blok writes: "We are the Scythians! We are the slit-eyed Asians! Try to wage war with us—you'll try no more!" In your opinion, what exactly was the ideology of "Scythianism" Blok and other Russian intellectuals were involved in during the years surrounding the revolution?*

That poem of Blok's is beautiful, but what it says is all wrong. First of all, the Scythians were an Iranian race. The discovery of the wheel, the anchor, and many other things have been attributed to them. It was a flourishing civilization, with ties to Greece, with a rich and unique culture. "Scythianism" is the Orient misinterpreted. Besides, even before Blok wrote that poem, even before Scythianism existed, this question, the fascination with the Orient, with primitive cultures, was in Dostoyevsky, in Tolstoy. Tolstoy and his love for the steppe. He lived in Bashkiria and he thought he was in the lands of the *Iliad*. Scythianism was a movement with an anti-European bent.

*So in some ways it was a particularly difficult moment in the search for Russian cultural "identity," the old question: Asian or European.*

You see, this issue is very, very complex in our literature. Take Gogol, perhaps our greatest writer. Such a genuine Ukrainian (and one mustn't forget the influence of the Ukrainian baroque, of Catholic culture on his art), such a devoted son of Russia. His relationship with the motherland is complex. He loves it and he mistreats it with love. He lives in Italy, he even knows which well in Rome has the best water. Remember how "Diary of a Madman" ends: "Take me! Give me a troika of steeds swift as the wind! Carry me out of this world! farther, farther [...] a forest races by with dark trees and a crescent moon; blue mist spreads under my feet; a string twangs in the mist; on one side the sea, on the other Italy; and there

I see some Russian huts." So, on one side, Italy, and on the other, the Russian hut, and the madman who thinks he's the King of Spain flies off in an out-of-control troika. The troika that later returns at the end of *Dead Souls*: "And you, Russia of mine, are not you also speeding like a troika which nought can overtake?" And the whole world is watching this bird-troika. And Gogol proudly declares that it wasn't built by the Germans. And this troika is contemporary with the railroads, the trains that he, Gogol, took all over Europe . . . You see, as our classics say, the Russian man, the young Russian, loves boundless freedom, for himself and for everyone else. And the steppe is freedom, open space, limitless. It is the motherland. And it's also the beginning of the Russian epic. Chekhov began with the steppe too, and although he called Gogol "king of the steppe," he thought that the Russian steppe still remained unsung. He was born in Taganrog, he came from the steppes. From the Kievan steppes. There weren't any Scythians, there were Greeks, and there were nomadic populations, some completely uncivilized, others who had their own culture, who knew how to work the land. When Pushkin went to Odessa he found himself in ancient sites, depicted long before in the *byliny*. But if Pushkin wrote in the poem *Poltava*, "Quiet is the Ukrainian night . . ."

Gogol, his great rival, writes in "A May Night": "Do you know the Ukrainian night? Oh, you do not know the Ukrainian night!" Already, Gogol was dreaming of the great epic of the steppe. And *Dead Souls* was born, this story of small men, petty landowners, a petty fraud, all people who want to earn relatively small sums and commit small crimes to this end—and everything is interspersed with panoramas of vast Russia, of the as-yet-unsung Russia. And so this vast, grand Russia, epic Russia, as strange as it may seem, winds up in Blok, the lyrical Blok who describes his country thus: "And sticking in the slushy gutter / The motley spokes can hardly gain . . ." And how can we forget Khlebnikov, who returns to the steppe and references Sviatoslav, his enemies drinking out of his skull? You see, the steppe is . . . it's Russia's untapped potential. And, of course, Esenin plays a part in this complicated issue as well. The strange, unexpected Esenin.

*You knew Esenin, no? When he was still in his "peasant" period, before the revolution.*

Yes, and I've written about the spats incident. When Zinaida Gippius asked him: "It seems you are wearing new gaiters?" and he replied, "They're *valenki*, madam." And they really were valenki. It was cold out, there was a terrible cold. Moreover, here in Russia, gaiters have never been popular. This episode took place in a very elegant house, a salon, the Muruzi House. At that time, we had this expression: "Merezhkovsky is at Dom Muruzi and he's looking for the divine spirit floor by floor . . ." Gippius . . . You know what Gippius means? It comes from the Greek *hippos*, horse. We called her hippo. She was a baroness, of German origin, Von Hippius, and there was a horse on their coat of arms. She was a very haughty woman. A good writer, with a tragic streak, like Vyacheslav Ivanov. But at the same time, an unrealized writer. Anyway, as far as haughtiness is concerned, the proudest Russian was without a doubt Mayakovsky. I remember him declaiming, "Wilson, I mean . . . Woodrow, you want a wheelbarrow of my blood?" Yes, Russia is a very strange country, where you can even ask the dead to rise. And it's even possible that they would . . . What was I talking about?

*Esenin. Esenin and Russia.*

Esenin wrote: "The old maple on one leg / guards blue Russia." It's very poetic. Fable-esque. Esenin returned to myth through Afanasiev's book which argues that folktales are based on myth, that folktales are stories about ancient gods . . . Then Esenin died . . . I remember—many years after Esenin's death, there was the war, his sister had been sent away . . . And some carpenters rebuilt Esenin's *izba*. Not for money. On their own initiative, as a gift. Then the noncommissioned officers were called back, and before leaving for the war many of them passed by and took a handful of earth from the yard of Esenin's house. To take with them, in the war. You see, Esenin was a man of the people. He drank. But here the people drink. Mayakovsky wrote about that too:

> So to say, if you had swapped bohemianism for class,
> there'd have been no bust-up,
> class'd have influenced
> your thinking.
> But does class quench its thirst with kvass?
> Class, too, is no fool when it comes to drinking.

# December 28

CIVIL WAR IN PETROGRAD, DEAD HORSES IN THE STREETS.
THE "SHIP OF FOOLS." THE SERAPION BROTHERS: LOTS
OF YOUNG PEOPLE, SOME IN THEIR TEENS. REVOLUTION
= DICTATORSHIP OF THE ACADEMY OF SCIENCES. MEY-
ERHOLD, THE OLDEST DIRECTOR IN THE WORLD. HIS AR-
CHIVES SAVED BY EISENSTEIN. TWO INSPECTORS GENERAL.
ZOSHCHENKO TURNS ON SOME DISCONCERTING LIGHTS.
BERLIN. A MISTREATED HAT. AN UPLIFTING SONG.

*Shall we try to pick up again where we left off? We were
up to 1917. You had returned to Petrograd after being
wounded in the war . . .*

Aleksey Maksimovich Gorky had gone back to Petrograd
before the revolution and had started the magazine *Leto-
pis* [Chronicle]. It was there that some of my reviews came
out. They were very harsh reviews. But I wasn't scared. I

was young. At the time Gorky was a liberal—very liberal—Democratic-Socialist. The magazine published many Bolsheviks too. Mayakovsky published some of his things there; Babel was in there too, early Babel with his wonderful stories, nothing like them since—I remember the one about the two old Chinese men: they go looking for women, one of them is impotent and a very kind prostitute heals him . . . then Babel took off down the Volga. After the revolution . . . Several plans came about. At the time I was on the editorial staff of the *Vestnik Iskusstv* [Herald of the Arts]. It was a newspaper, and we didn't have anything to paste it on the walls. So we put the papers in water, and the cold alone made them stick to the walls, you just had to be careful not to freeze your hands too. Those were hard times . . . Nobody shoveled the snow on the street, on Nevsky, I remember, there was only a little path that was practicable, which wound through tall mounds of snow. And at night a clarinetist would pass through, I think he was from the Mariinsky Theater, and he played his instrument. People gave him a lot of money, he played well. In that period, after the revolution, I spent a great deal of time with Gorky. He had scurvy, and he would rinse out his mouth with an infusion of oak bark. Yes, they were very hard times. Near the Troitsky Bridge,

I remember, a dead horse lay for a long time. It was there for a while, then people cut it up and everybody took away a piece for themselves.

*And at about the same time Esenin wrote, in a poem, "Black crows, their wings spread out like sails, were eating its flesh."*

Esenin wasn't the only one to write about it. Mayakovsky wrote "A horse fell" . . . and at the same time, in Moscow, Gorky published a feuilleton about a fallen horse. Yes, at that time horses didn't last long. But we had big plans . . . When 1921 came—and it came with a horrible famine—I remember that Gorky's son, a good boy, talented, brought a cart or two with horse heads to Petrograd. Evidently the rest of those horses was somewhere, but we got the heads. That was when Tikhonov, fresh from the war, wrote:

> Ships call on us only by chance, and freight trains
> Bring cargoes out of habit, that is all;
> Just count the men belonging to my country—
> How many dead will answer to the call!

On the corner of Nevsky and the Moika, not far from the house where Pushkin died, there's a huge building. The "House of Arts" opened there. Grin lived there, Shaginyan, Gumilyov, Miklashevsky, a good painter unknown outside Russia, Pyast lived there too. And I went to live there as well. There were lots of us. Sometimes we didn't even know each other. They gave us a little money. In that period Gorky wanted to create a publishing house, "Universal Literature," which would publish writers from every era. All of world literature, from *Gilgamesh*, say, to Leonid Andreyev. The books were all translated, and translated well, but most of them were only published several years later. I don't have them, they wouldn't all fit in my house. It was a way to help and organize writers. And it was because of this opportunity that the House of Arts held translation courses. They would serve tea, some bread, and a little something else. And the group that assembled in that translators' studio was wonderful.

*Who gave the lessons?*

There was Zamyatin teaching, Chukovsky; I held lessons too. One time when there was a terrible cold, just like today in Moscow, in fact, the only one who showed up was Blok.

*With professors of that stature they must not have been simple lessons on translation . . .*

No, of course not, they were lectures, free lectures. Blok talked about art, the revolution, the intelligentsia. I spoke on literature. Sometimes there were only five people in a huge room. It used to be the dining room of Yeliseyev, an extremely wealthy merchant who had emigrated. The building where the House of Arts was, in fact, had been his house—enormous, three floors, with a library and music hall. It's the Yeliseyev who left the big grocery store on Gorky Prospekt in Moscow. He was famous, in his time: in France they gave him the Legion of Honor for his method of aging wines. He was an expert oenologist. And the buildings he constructed in Petersburg and Moscow have lasted. Tolstoy called them "temples of sausage." But in our time Yeliseyev was already gone, there was no more sausage, only the house remained. And that's where we had our meetings. And that's where we formed—actually, it formed itself, right after the House opened—the "Serapion Brothers": Zoshchenko, Vsevolod Ivanov, Lunts, Pozner—

then very young (later, he returned to Paris)—me, Fedin, Nikitin, Elizaveta Polonskaia, Tikhonov. Tikhonov joined after the group had already formed. He was coming from the war. He wore a long military overcoat, he'd been in the Red Army cavalry. He hadn't published anything yet, but he brought some excellent poems from the war. We were all very young, some of us were just boys . . . Who else was there? There was Slonimsky, he was the grandson of a publisher, and he was a good writer, not great but good, and a good person. Because of the cold, he was always in bed, under his overcoat, and who knows why but the Serapion Brothers always met at his place, in his room, around his bed, instead of in the big room. And for some reason, something that, I remember, amused Gorky to no end, in Slonimsky's room there was a vent that dripped water. Apparently a pipe had broken somewhere . . . Anyway, the atmosphere was . . . Olga Forsh called the House of Arts a "ship of fools" . . .

*It was Gorky's initiative to create the House of Arts. What was his relationship to the Serapion "Brotherhood?"*

Gorky was a friend. He would come often . . . He was a multifaceted man, a great talent, with an incredible memory. He could recite a Chekhov story with every punctuation mark. One time he ran into an old acquaintance at our place, someone from his town, and he listed every single person who used to live there . . .

*What was the role of Zamyatin's teachings in the Serapions' practice and choices?*

Zamyatin was very important for the brotherhood. He was a very strong man, and a good novelist, just look at *The Islanders*. And he was a good engineer too. He was the one, you know, who built the "Krasin," the ship that saved Nobile. Zamyatin was called when the Nobile disaster happened, and if he had come back to Russia he would have been the one to save Nobile, on his ship. After emigrating, Zamyatin never wrote again . . .

*And you held lessons alongside Zamyatin, Blok . . . That shows that you weren't simply a member of the "brotherhood," but somehow an authority for the other "brothers."*

The fact is, I was older. I'd already been to war, for a long time, I had been wounded. Anyway, you could say that there were two groups within the brotherhood. At the center of one was Vsevolod Ivanov. Who, I must say, started out as a great writer. When he joined us he was fresh from the war—actually, no, he was coming from Siberia, from the partisan struggle. One day Gorky told me that a guy with a red beard had shown up, his coat singed, with a wide face, Kyrgyz perhaps, and that this person was looking for him. And he told me to get some money for him, you never knew, I might run into him. I was astonished: "But, Aleksey Maksimovich, that seems highly unlikely . . ." But I got some money, and that very day, on Nevsky, at the corner of Sadovaya, I saw a man with a reddish beard and a singed coat. I stopped him and said: "Are you Ivanov?" And he: "How do you know?" I replied: "Gorky knows how to paint a picture." I gave him the money. Then he and Gorky met, they talked. And Vsevolod Ivanov wrote a wonderful story; the next one, however, was bad. He was maybe the oldest out of all of us. He wrote war stories. His father was a Cossack who, in his time, who knows why, had studied for a while at the Lazarev Institute of Foreign Languages. Vsevolod Ivanov came from a Cossack *stanitsa* where there was no stone left upon another . . . All of us, at the time, thought he would become the Russian Balzac.

*So, Ivanov was the head of this group . . .*

No, for heavens' sake, nobody was at the head of anything. There were no heads. And, in general, back then it was easier to call the Chairman of the Supreme Soviet than it is to get a hold of the Housing Office today—you can call for hours without anybody answering. One time I had to call Sverdlov about a very important matter, he told me that I should come by at a certain time. I got there, he let me in, and the first thing he said was: "Shklovsky, you have no idea what a great pleasure it is for an old revolutionary to be able to write and take notes. That wasn't possible before. You had to keep everything in your head. And now, you see, I've taken your documents (I had just gotten back from Ukraine, I had all sorts of cards) and I can see everything that happens . . ." It was a period in which everything got done. Once, the Neva flooded and, like in the times of Onegin, we saw a huge barge on Mokhovaya Street. In short, we felt like it was the end and the beginning of the world at the same time. The white nights, then, were whiter than they've ever been since. Because our heads were clear, our eyes were fresh. And hope. What hope? No less and no more than of rebuilding the entire world. We believed that there would be revolution not only in, let's say, Hungary or Germany, but also, inevitably, in France. We weren't thinking of Italy at the time, but in Spain, yes, there would be revolution, we were sure of it.

*But what did revolution mean to you then?*

Well, for example, we thought: there will be the dictatorship of the Academy of Sciences. Why are you laughing? Exactly that: the dictatorship of the Academy of Sciences, or rather, the dictatorship of art. The freedom of art. Look, I'll try to explain it this way: there was a train headed for the future and we were pushing and shoving one another to get on. But we were convinced that it would come . . .

*How long was the Serapion Brotherhood active?*

Three or four years. As for me, I left. I also abandoned Opoyaz. And anyway, you see, you grow up, you mature. Nikolai Nikitin, for example, was a talented writer, who wrote good things—then came the first successes, the first money, the first new people, the first women. Tikhonov, who impressed us all with his skill, fought in the Finnish War, and later became—how should I put this, not a bureaucrat, but someone who wanted to prove that he was in on everything. Gruzdev wrote a biography of Gorky. Only the beginning, of course. It would be extremely difficult to finish, but it should be done, it would be very interesting . . . Gorky, at a certain point, left, he went abroad, and after that, I too, by chance, found myself abroad. I've already mentioned that story. I was supposed to testify at a trial. A political trial. I wasn't a Socialist-Revolutionary. It was a trial against the Socialist-Revolutionaries. I refused to participate. How? I was young then. I went over the ice, crossed a frozen segment of the Gulf of Finland and ended up in Finland. And then I ended up in Berlin. I had no ties there. I'm not political. And the acquaintances and friends I had there were Bolsheviks. There was Larisa Reisner, the wonderful Meyerhold came with the young Zinaida Raikh . . .

*Before moving on to your memories of Berlin, would you mind saying something about Meyerhold?*

Meyerhold was the oldest director in the world. I fought with him. We fought about Gogol, *The Inspector General.*

The mise-en-scène was brilliant, but I didn't like the fact that the mayor's wife—played by Raikh—was such a beautiful woman. Because she was so beautiful it was painful. I remember the set of *The Inspector*, gorgeous: at that time it was unbelievably easy to find the most precious Venetian crystals on the street. And this lavishness . . . You see Meyerhold's mises-en-scène didn't take the author into account, they passed over him. But sometimes they hit the mark. For example, with Ostrovsky's *The Forest*. Raikh was in that as well. The priest, I remember, had gold hair, made out of tinsel. And you know how it ended, what the comedy's conclusion was? Schastlivtsev and Neschastlivtsev need to find a tragic actress . . . They find one and finally all together they can create a new type of theater: the theater of Meyerhold . . . As strange as it is, this fantastic show with dancing sailors, balalaika players, this crazy spectacle was successful with audiences. What else can I say about Meyerhold? That he lived and died a Bolshevik.

*I understand what you mean, but bringing up Meyer-hold's death can't not bring to mind the atrociously unjust way in which he died, and also, a question as obvious as it is unavoidable: in the face of all this—persecution, disappearances, death—what did people do? Were they afraid, did they protest, react somehow?*

They were afraid, of course. But Meyerhold left behind an enormous archive. When everything was over, this archive was discovered in Eisenstein's dacha. Eisenstein had never said anything to anyone. How he was able to take all that material from a guarded house, I really can't figure out. And he never talked to anybody about it, so that word wouldn't get out, and thus the archive was preserved.

*I'm sorry, I interrupted you—you were talking about Meyerhold's productions.*

You see, Meyerhold was very indebted to Stanislavski, on the one hand, and on the other, he was a madman who let his students put on the production only to then interrupt it and turn it on its head. And the great thing is that it gave you the impression that the work was perfectly comfortable in that position. It's as if to start, Meyerhold first needed to stage the work in an ordinary, traditional manner.

*And Meyerhold the man?*

He was charming, inventive, he knew how to be poor with grace. My wife, Serafima Gustavovna, often went to his house. One anecdote: Meyerhold had a ruined stomach, he suffered from diarrhea. And his house, one day, was full of guests, there were people everywhere, even on the floor. He, Meyerhold, first went to the bathroom on tiptoe, then he strode by with long, magisterial steps, then he went on all fours, with newspaper pages in his mouth. He was someone who could make a show out of anything.

*And you, Viktor Borisovich, do you remember another famous, sensational production of* The Inspector General *in the '20s? I'm thinking of Terentyev's show, which was probably also the last public appearance of such a gifted artist, who also died prematurely, it seems, in Stalin's purges.*

Terentyev, there's a man who's been forgotten . . . On the Moika, right across from the house where Akhmatova lived, there was the "House of the Press." It was there that Terentyev put on *The Inspector General*. The set, I remember, was made of transparent material. Bobchinsky and

Dobchinsky were played by two women. The merchant Abdulin was a Tatar and he sang in Tatar. In the end, when the real inspector's arrival is announced, he enters, removes his cap, and we discover that it's Khlestakov again. It was a wonderful show. Terentyev had also staged a text by a Proletarian writer, now I can't remember who—I remember that at some point there was a woman dying; she was put on the table and she lay there, dead, when all of a sudden she starts talking and describing the situation. I remember that even the audience was scared . . . You see, they say that sometimes scientists play this game: forget reality, anything is possible, don't be afraid to invent. Bohr, I am quite sure it was him, once said to me about an idea: it's not crazy enough to be true. And old Tolstoy said that the reasonable is impoverished whereas everything that's foolish is rich, fecund. In art this absolute freedom, freedom from assistance, from external support, is indispensable. For example, opera, at one time, was financed, today we have the Bolshoi Theater which, for heaven's sake, we all love and respect, but . . . But we were talking about the Serapion Brothers, right?

*Yes. You said that Ivanov had one group. And the other?*

The other one was very, very "leftist."

*And that was the one, let's not say headed by you, but open to your influence?*

I wouldn't know. I don't think they were crazy enough to be open to my influence. In this second group there was Pozner, Lunts, a very interesting writer who died suddenly, very young—even as a young man he wrote some nice theater pieces. Gorky had arranged a trip to Spain for him. Lunts died suddenly, en route. And he already had a very sad work among his things: *Journey on a Hospital Bed.* There was also Elizaveta Polonskaia. There was Kaverin, who had started off his writing career very well. I remember one of his stories from that period: two people have a cellar and they want to expand it a little. They begin digging, they dig and dig and they come to the end of the world. They find themselves in a strange space, like a folded-up polygon. And where is the world? They walk around, they keep going, at a certain point they see the world rolling toward them in the form of a barrel. And the story ends there. Kaverin was full of ideas, of discoveries . . . Eh, at that time these inventions were easy, very easy . . .

*And which group was Zoshchenko in?*

Zoshchenko was between the one and the other. He joined our group. He was handsome. He had a nice physique. Straight legs. He was easygoing and quiet. But he was always getting offended, even though we all liked him and nobody teased him. He'd been an officer in the army, he'd received major military awards, then he had worked for the police and finally he ended up with us. His satires and comic stories were real. I remember his story "Poverty." They install electricity, and put lightbulbs in the house. But the light reveals that the house is ugly, a mess, in need of repair. And they start improving things, but it's so difficult that instead of going on with the renovation they get rid of the lights. Or this other amazing story: a man is walking on the outskirts of Piter and sees on a building, up on the third floor, a bronze plaque that indicates the level of the water during the flood of 1824. He's perplexed. He asks some people nearby and they tell him: we had to put the plaque there so that nobody would steal it. Zoshchenko's stories, his irony, his jabs at bad people, a bad past . . . But the people who built the world wanted that world to be as if it were designed, they wanted Potemkin villages. And when they started reading Zoshchenko, they tore him apart. That had a big impact on him, because he was fully convinced that he was a realist. Like Shostakovich. Shostakovich expected *Pravda* to publish an essay of his analyzing the score for *The Nose*. You see, this is the situation of the artist who's ahead of his time. Even if it must be said that, sometimes, his time understands him. Zoshchenko, for example, was absolutely loved by the people. And when he died, there were tons of people at his funeral. He was buried between two sand dunes, in the bare sand, and on the grave there's a stone in the shape of a book, which just says "Zoshchenko." It was the workers in the Sestroreck factory who made him that monument. They loved him.

*Zoshchenko's name is linked—in a negative way, unfortunately—to Zhdanov, who signed the famous resolution against Zoshchenko, and Akhmatova, in 1946. Who was Zhdanov, Viktor Borisovich?*

He was someone who knew how to play the piano.

*But as far as you know was he a literary critic, was he involved at all with literature?*

No.

*Yet he was destined to become the star of Soviet cultural politics in the postwar period.*

You know something? One time Zoshchenko came to Moscow, he went to a hotel, but there were no rooms. He settled in a common area. And people were astonished that he was still around, still in circulation. Stalin . . . He was an atrocious phenomenon. But it's not possible for a man like that to make it by chance. And you can't put all the blame on a single person. Zhdanov was a civil servant. At some point they told him: Write. There's a legend about the Zoshchenko affair. One day, Stalin was on vacation at his daughter's; he found one of his books, read it, and it unsettled him. He was seeing the world in another way.

*This detail, legendary or no, confirms the peculiar, appalling arbitrariness of the "mechanism." And if Stalin had found a different book that day? To use an absurd example, a book by Mayakovsky . . .*

He probably liked Mayakovsky.

*In recompense, Lenin didn't like Mayakovsky. At least the*

poem "150,000,000," *since—remember?—he recommended against its publication . . .*

As far as that poem is concerned, you see, the mistake is also Mayakovsky's. Because there the poet isn't speaking with his voice, but with the voice of the politician. He wants to represent the whole country . . . To think that here, to this day, a collection of Mayakovsky's love poetry has never been published. Why take love from Mayakovsky? And here, anyway, I believe, and in Italy as well, kids are horrified by what they have to study in school: Pushkin, Gogol, Mayakovsky . . . They read them, they have to read them for exams, so they don't like them . . . And revolution transforms the world, it creates a new world, but it finds itself still in the old one . . . But what was I talking about?

*Going in chronological order, though with many whims and digressions, we had come to your Berlin days. You were in Berlin for almost two years, right?*

I was. And in Berlin there were—or they passed through— many of my friends and acquaintances. There was Maya- kovsky, Eisenstein (though by the time I got there he was already gone), there was Igor Severyanin, there was even Nemirovich-Danchenko. Bely was there, bitter and sad after his affair with anthroposophy went sour. There were many painters in the avant-garde. One time I went to see an exhibit and I was astonished: it was like being in Moscow . . . Berlin was going downhill. I'm not much for politics, I'm no politician, but I think that if at the time there hadn't been that division which later emerged—neither of their volition nor of ours—between Social-Democrats and Bolsheviks, Berlin wouldn't have become fascist. But I saw the fascists, with my own eyes. Long before, after the defeat, when we had disbanded the army, they shaved the backs of their heads. And when someone shaves his head it means a war is about to begin. Germany is a very tenacious, precise country. For us Russians it's incomprehensible, even if enviable in many ways: they know how to work, they're precise in their work. I remember I bought a hat and in the pension where I was living—at the time Erenburg was living there too—there was a doorman who usually opened the door by pushing a button, after checking to see who it was. One night, I ring the bell and I see him get up and come to open the door himself. He was holding a tray, and on the tray there was a hat. "Young man," he says to me, "do you see this hat? I've been wearing it for four years. But you, you just bought your hat, and look what condition it's been reduced to! Do you think you can treat things this way?" Eh, sure, it wasn't his business, but it's also true that things don't like to be treated badly. Berlin . . . Remizov, who also lived in Berlin at that time—and, you know, was supposed to return to Russia, I was supposed to go and pick him up at the station myself—Remizov wrote: "*Krug* is a German word. There's nothing to feel superior about. And *malyar* is a German word too. We shouldn't consider ourselves superior." Anyway, you see, everyone is made in his own way, and I couldn't last in that climate for long. Of course, at the time I didn't know what was going to happen. Gorky and Mayakovsky actively took on my case, and, moreover, I hadn't done anything. Long story short, I went back to Russia. Water, as they say, is water for the fish but not for the birds. In Berlin, I never wrote for the White papers, I didn't have ties of any kind, connections, not even with people who spoke Russian well. For a while, in Berlin, I lived with Gorky, who in that period was also waiting for another revolution, but he didn't believe in the peasants, he believed in the proletariat. You see, men expect miracles from themselves, remember what I told you about Filonov? But we weren't able to walk on water . . . It takes patience, and lots of testing the water in the meantime. I suppose that's how it has to be. I remember a great writer who said: "Don't give up desperation." Because one could say that desperation is indispensable. It helps not to think that it's your neighbor keeping you from being happy. Man's principal enemy is his heart. Yuri Olesha wrote wonderfully about this. One time, he wrote, he suddenly heard a strange noise. He asked his grandmother what it could be: it was his heartbeat. It was the first time he had heard his heart beating. And from that moment on he listened to it for the rest of his life. We need to listen to our heart, without ruining it. Art always poses man the task, the problem of the future. Don Quixote, as Dostoyevsky said, isn't guilty of anything. He's cultured, he doesn't exploit his mad glory, he's intelligent, he doesn't need anything, it's just that he isn't able to transform the world *instantly*. But humanity needs that. You see, the Russian term *poka chto* is ugly, I don't like it, this one is nice: *nichego*. One time, Tolstoy wrote down a song that the Russian soldiers in the Caucasus used to sing. A lovely, difficult song. Wait, I'll sing it to you:

In a word, it's terrible
Or certainly not quite bearable
Well, let's just say it's nothing.

And this word, *nichego*, which in Russia is used so often, whose exact meaning nobody knows, in actuality means many things—it means that one is not yet defeated. And that we go on, even if it's very difficult.

# December 29

THE BIRTH OF SOVIET CINEMA IS COMPARED TO THE CRE-
ATION OF THE WORLD. THE LETATLIN: A DREAMING MA-
CHINE. THE WEAPON OF PATIENCE. MAYAKOVSKY DIDN'T
WANT DEBTS. DIGRESSION ON PASTERNAK'S POETRY, BUL-
GAKOV'S NOVELS. SHKLOVSKY BEGINS TO WORK IN CINEMA,
HE WRITES INTERTITLES AND THEN SCRIPTS. HE MEETS
EISENSTEIN. WHAT WAS THE ROLE OF DISHES IN THE OCTO-
BER REVOLUTION? SOME FILMS SHKLOVSKY WROTE: *BY THE
LAW, BED AND SOFA, MININ AND POZHARSKY*. SHKLOVSKY
TEARS APART TARKOVSKY'S *ANDREI RUBLEV*. AN UNUSUAL
EDITING JOB. AN EVEN MORE UNUSUAL WRITING JOB.

*For today's conversation, Viktor Borisovich, I'd like to propose
a topic that I know is dear to you: film. You witnessed, one
could say, the birth of the great Soviet cinema firsthand . . .*

Imagine the creation of the world. The world doesn't exist yet: it's being born. Some of the people who were working in pre-revolutionary Russia, good writers, good men in cinema, many of them had left, very few remained. Only in a second phase did some of them start coming back. The post-revolutionary cinema was a cinema that was learning how to be cinema. Almost all the new directors, before then, had never worked in the cinema. They came from painting, from sculpture, from medicine. And it wasn't like that just in film. It was the era. We young people suddenly found ourselves on an open shore. And we dreamed. There were architects, like Melnikov, designing buildings with enormous interior spaces, with stairs that passed through rings—wonderful projects, but we didn't have the materials to accomplish them properly. In those years nice houses were built, interesting constructions, but made with shoddy materials. What to do? There was nothing, in the cities people were even plowing the patches of land between the buildings trying to grow potatoes. There was hunger. And with that great, vast hunger, we young people, whose stomachs were by no means full even before the revolution, raced to create the world. Just think of Tatlin's invention, the Letatlin, on the tower of the old monastery, where the Aleksandr Nevsky cemetery is. The Letatlin was a flying machine. It was a copy of a bird, it had a very light metal structure. But it couldn't fly. It could only dream. It was the dream of flight. The dream of a great man. The same Tatlin designed the famous building that was supposed to stand at an incline and rotate on itself at the same time. It was a monument to the October Revolution. I saw the model, now it's at the Architecture Museum. I don't know if it's intact, if the mechanism still works, but that tower gives an idea of the magnitude of his dream. I've been told that many architecture projects from that period were built later by Finnish architects. They have the materials and the desire to do it. You see, it was as if we were all in uncharted territory, you could do anything, invent the Letatlin for example. I remember that it was exhibited at the Writers' Union. It was very beautiful. Some people came from Denmark to film it. But they wouldn't let them. Because, you see, the Letatlin wasn't on the Soviet regime's list of works, it was as if it didn't exist. And Tatlin was not liked. They said that the place where the Letatlin was had been recently painted. The Danes responded that it wasn't a big deal, they had come from Denmark for the sole purpose of filming it, they would fix it afterward, repaint, but they still didn't let them do it. Later, after a great deal of effort, Konstantin Simonov managed to put together a Tatlin exhibit. And the press started talking about him again. You see, an artist's most important weapon is patience. An artist can't expect to be liked immediately. Picasso, for example, possessed the gift of patience, Chagall had it too . . .

*Perhaps poets need it too, sometimes. In your opinion, for example, did Mayakovsky possess this weapon?*

No, not always. But there was another problem, you see. Mayakovsky allowed himself to be seduced by theory, an incorrect theory, about the end of art. Yet he was a poet, a great poet. His theme was love. But they tried to prove to him that this wasn't valid, constructive. And Mayakovsky lived, in some ways, a double life.

*Do you mean, in other words, that Mayakovsky had two sides, that he didn't believe in what he wrote?*

No, Mayakovsky believed in it, always. He lived extremely modestly. He scrupulously kept track of his expenses and income, he didn't want to spend more than he had, because the day could always come when you absolutely needed money, no matter what. Debts are a burden, they restrict you. And he didn't want to be in debt to anyone. When he writes "Pro Eto," Mayakovsky defends the right to poetry. And you see, this existence of art at multiple levels simultaneously is our secret. Mayakovsky wanted to be liked, liked right away. To be liked, first and foremost, by the Revolution. He wanted the workers to like him, on their terms. He wanted another audience, another public. I believe that all the great poets have two sides. Just think of Dante, who creates his *Inferno* and puts in all the great men of Florence, all the popes. And in *The Inferno* there's a revision of everything, of every value, even though Dante wants to go down in history as a champion of Catholicism.

*Seeing as the discussion has returned to poets, I'd like to take advantage of this to fill some serious gaps in my questions. I haven't asked you, for example, about Pasternak.*

Yes, I remember, I remember Pasternak well. For some time we lived in the same house, on Lavrushinsky Lane.

We both published in *LEF*. Then he started writing for other magazines and I remember Mayakovsky saying: "They took one of our own." I like Pasternak as a poet, as a complex poet who, in my opinion—though he would get offended when I told him this—had taken a different poetic path, following Igor Severyanin, that is, writing poetry that introduces the everyday into the aesthetic sphere. Pasternak, let's say, writes that a skating rink is a giant mirror, or he compares raindrops to cufflinks . . . There's nature and then there's the level of the intimate, the everyday. In other words, Pasternak was able to introduce objects into poetry that previously had been excluded. He was very good friends with Mayakovsky. After Volodya's death he wrote a couple things about him. One was published, have you read it? Later, though, he said that Mayakovsky didn't exist, as a poet. I argued with him, actually there was never a real disagreement—it was simply that our paths diverged. So, while Mayakovsky was a friend, a close friend, Pasternak and I never "saw eye to eye."

*Viktor Borisovich, I'd like to devote a little more time to other great figures of Soviet literature. I realize we haven't spoken much about the prose writers. Do you like Bulga-kov?*

Bulgakov is a wonderful, incomparable writer. When I read, for example, *The Master and Margarita* . . . I fall apart like clothes in the rain and humidity. In the novel, Bulgakov describes the building where we writers had a kind of restaurant, which overlooked the street. And there, a few feet away, Mandelstam lived behind one wall, Platonov lived across the way. Mayakovsky lived in a room. For a while Pasternak lived there. Shostakovich was there. It was the old Herzen House, on Tverskoy Boulevard—on one end there was the Danish embassy and on the other were the rooms where the writers lived. What am I getting at? That it wasn't such a bad or insignificant era. Not at all. There were still the Futurists, there was still Opoyaz. But it must also be said that Bulgakov was a great artist. *The Master and Margarita* is a very strong work, especially the beginning: Pilate with his headache, the apostle looking for a knife to kill someone . . . I like the end less though, when the Master meets Christ they have nothing to say to each other. Because Christ is better informed, he has all the news, he's more interested and involved in the problems of the world.

And there are witches in the novel . . . When I was young, a long time ago, we were all interested in the topic, there was a whole literature on it. No, I'm not talking about folktales, it was scientific research, volumes and volumes of it. Bosch, for us, was completely comprehensible. From an ideological perspective, *The Master and Margarita* is related to Goethe's early works, and to Hegel. But I found Bulgakov's other novel, *A Dead Man's Memoir*, more striking.

*Since I certainly won't have time to ask you about every single prose writer, I'd like to at least ask you this question: who was, in your opinion, the writer who did the most for Russian prose of our century, for the language of Soviet narrative?*

I couldn't say. The official verdict, in my opinion mistaken, claims it was Gorky. That's not true. Gorky was a romantic when he started out, later on paying more attention to the realm of the everyday, and there are perhaps traces of this later phase in Ivanov. I am of the opinion that, even if for a short amount of time, Andrei Bely's prose mattered a great deal.

*All right, then let's return to the topic "of the day." Why did you, Viktor Borisovich, begin to work in cinema?*

The story goes like this: I wasn't teaching anymore—as I've said, I had some troubles because of formalism. And in that particular period I had a child on the way.

*So, you came back from Berlin, in late 1923, if I'm not mistaken. And you moved to Moscow? When?*

Look, I don't remember. Go ahead and write that I don't remember. Anyway, when I came back from Berlin, I went to the NKVD for my documents and they told me: "Don't go to Leningrad. Because we know. They don't." They were referring to my case, which had been closed by Sverdlov. So I thought I wouldn't tempt fate and fortune and I stayed in Moscow. As I said, I was about to have a child. I had no money. My wife couldn't go to the hospital because I hadn't paid the union fees. I was told that you could make money, anyone could make money, in cinema. So I went, I went to the Third Factory, the one that provided the title for one of my books. There was . . . Actually, no, it was like this: I'd asked for help from a writer, who, moreover, never loaned out money. He was the one who suggested that I work in the cinema. So I went, albeit reluctantly. I said I needed money. They didn't give me any right away, naturally. They told me: sit down and write the titles for his film, when you're finished we'll pay you. I sat down and began to work. I turned the projector by hand. And from then on I kept working in cinema. And I wanted to understand what it was, what it was about. It simply didn't exist. Films were often shot in these small ateliers that looked like photography studios. They had to start from scratch. Besides that, the most important thing is that there were no directors. There was nothing, just the movie houses abandoned by their owners, many of whom had emigrated. Some of these former owners were smart people, good craftsmen. The former owner of the Third Factory for example, Kozlovsky, who was a camera operator himself. You know what he was like? They were shooting a scene with a bear. The animal jumped on the actor with a menacing look. And Kozlovsky, who was directing, said: "Keep filming the bear, for heaven's sake!" The bear was killed. "You ruined my shot!" On another occasion, he was shooting a scene with wolves, a wolf lunged at the cameraman, and Kozlovsky says: "Don't stop shooting!" These people were absolutely possessed by the fever of cinema. They were like the first aviators . . .

*How long were you writing intertitles?*

After the titles they had me doing scripts. I rewrote scripts by other screenwriters. I wrote with incredible speed. Then I got fed up with that job. I wrote my own script. It's a film that everyone has forgotten today: *The Wings of a Serf*. But I know in the West it had a fairly wide distribution. And so, in short, I kept working in cinema.

*Where you met figures who are now legendary . . .*

I can tell you in two words who Sergei Mikhailovich Eisenstein was. He studied at the Architecture Institute, he was going to become an architect, he wanted to build houses, but he went on to the theater, the most "left-wing" theater at the time, and there, for the production of Ostrovsky's *The Wiseman*, he made a short film that was put into the show. That was how, in a completely unexpected way, Eisenstein became a film director. And then Pudovkin was an engineer. He'd gone to war, he'd been in prison. He shot a short film on Pavlov's theory of conditioned reflexes. Pavlov saw it, he liked it. Anyway, Pudovkin also ended up in cinema completely by chance. Eisenstein went to the First Factory to do a test shot but it was lousy, mediocre. The second one wasn't any better. It was bad film. For the third and forth tries, cameramen and workers got involved, and the director of the First Factory, Mikhin, also lent a hand; he was a man who should have a world patent for the invention of the movable background, made with molding and plywood. That became the film *Strike*.

*Could you tell us something about Eisenstein the man?*

I feel entitled to do so as someone who was his friend during his lifetime, and because I've studied his archive. He was a man who knew how to move but couldn't dance. Broad-chested, his reddish hair always standing on end, young and cheerful, with an incredible, exceptional memory and mental ability. He'd studied Japanese, but I don't think he spoke it. But he knew the theory of painting to a T. He was an excellent painter, he painted every frame of his films, he was a great theorist of painting. His works were published in three volumes, but there are still many other studies on the theory of montage that ought to be published, and they're full of his sketches. See, I'm afraid of repeating myself on Eisenstein. I've written a book about him that has been translated into several languages . . . He was your typical great man. And he was also a poor man who didn't know it, who paid no attention to his own poverty. His father lived in Latvia, the old government was still there, the Eisensteins were rich, they owned multiple houses. But he didn't go back. He didn't leave because in the early years of his work, he had found freedom. Yes, he was a Letatlin, a machine that was able to take flight in the new Soviet Russia.

*And Eisenstein on the set?*

He never went near the camera, he never checked the frames. He didn't want to meddle with the camera work. He would design the frame, drawing it in every minute detail, or, for example, he would get involved with the makeup and so on, but once they started filming he everyone do their work, let Tisse do his work.

*What kind of relationship did he have with the actors?*

He didn't care for them. Eisenstein didn't like working with actors. He dreamed of having Ulanova, the ballerina, act for him. He said of her: "Now that's what I call an actress." His ideal actor was whomever he hadn't worked with. No, he wasn't fond of actors, even though he worked with some great pros. In general, if he could have, Eisenstein would have shot much more film, so he would have more footage to choose from. That was what he wanted most of all. And I must say that, there at the Factory, he was the favorite of the set workers. Because he didn't give them a drawing of the set design, he gave them a blueprint. He was well versed in these things, he had his architectural background. And the workers built the sets twice as fast for him as they did for any other director. The administrators, the heads of the cinema factory, were actually a little afraid of Sergei Mikhailovich. Even later, when he ran into some trouble, some ideological "fiascoes," as we would say, the administration continued to respect him. And Eisenstein, who was incredibly young, there at the factory he was always the oldest, the "captain." At the screening of *October*, Krupskaya, Lenin's widow, said: "It's very interesting, but I don't know if dishes played such a big part in the October Revolution." And at the premiere of *October* the audience was disappointed, they didn't like the film, they grumbled. I remember Pudovkin came up to me and said: "How I wish I had, what I'd give, for a flask of that energy. From now on everyone who was in the theater, including us, will work in a different way . . ."

*And you, personally, what do you think of those notorious dishes?*

Eisenstein doesn't care for the object in itself, what interests him is the reciprocal interaction of objects and ideas. To speak in formalist terms, in Eisenstein the word as such doesn't exist. And it's precisely his objects that demonstrate how art as such comes from the collision of opposing concepts and structures. That art isn't structure, but the conflict of structures. Art is the catastrophe of structures. And if one can say that imagination is better than reality, art is even better, because it's the dream of every structure's collapse and at the same time the dream of the construction of new structures.

*And, in this dream, what role did the technique of montage have for Eisenstein?*

We were at the initial phase of montage then, montage was a continual discovery, the directors didn't know exactly what it was about yet. There was Kuleshov, a former painter, an educated man with exceptional talent, who had his own particular destiny in the history of world cinema. This man taught the art of montage. To the young directors, the young cameramen, even to Vertov. And all this, you see, happened in the next room, a few feet away from where, perhaps, Eisenstein was working. It was an atmosphere of communal exploration. What did Kuleshov do? He didn't give practical demonstrations, but he talked about the "Kuleshov effect." That is, if you film an actor's face and surround it with shots of the most disparate content, according to whatever is put around it, the actor's face will be read differently every time. As if a completely extraneous word from one sentence were put in another sentence. Montage, the issue of who had first invented the new montage was the cause of the fight between Eisenstein and Vertov. Eisenstein wrote a very elegant article about it. Do you remember Gogol's

*Inspector General*, when Bobchinsky and Dobchinsky come to announce the inspector's arrival, all out of breath, each wanting to be the one to give the news and at the same time arguing over which one was the first to say "Eh"? Eisenstein's article was called "'Eh!' On the Purity of Film Language." The issue, therefore, was who had created the new montage. Eisenstein joked that his name began with an *E* and therefore the credit should go to him. But he was kidding, of course. It was the right time, the era, to speak that "Eh!" It's time that crowns the kings. Eisenstein said that he had been invented by the revolution. Yes, the revolution created him, invented him, and then it crushed him. I saw the *Battleship Potemkin* dossier with my own eyes. There's a short script, the original one, unfinished, and there's also a half-sheet with the fine the director had to pay for having spent more than the allocated budget. And he overspent only by a small amount. Everyone marveled at the success, the glory of that film. When they showed *Chapayev* to the director of a movie theater, he said, "Sure, that would play all right for a few clubs." It's hard to foresee, to see success. With some films they throw events, they spend a ton of money, and nothing comes out of it . . . But I was talking about Eisenstein, about the issue of montage. Vertov, one could say, would go a little overboard. In his films there's a multiplicity that's hard to follow. In film jargon this is called "camera abuse." Look, in cinema, as in every other art, to create the effect of sound there has to be silence first. To create the effect of surprise everything beforehand has to be taken for granted. You have to create a temple before you can destroy it. Like the Gospel says, "I can build and then destroy." Build the world and then destroy it—shamans can do that too, but to comprehend and give meaning to the destiny of creation and destruction, only the artist can do that. Take Tolstoy: he starts off with a description of a serene, carefree woman, Anna Karenina, and a carefree young officer who's satisfied with himself, and then he brings everything down, he destroys what he has built, and in this destruction he brings out and exposes the mechanisms of humanity.

*You've had a long and prolific career as a screenwriter. Somewhere I also saw that you wrote a manual on* How to Write Scripts. *Would you like to say something about this work, the conclusions you've drawn from it?*

We didn't have this skill, the profession of screenwriting. Because visual representation is without time. You can show ten, a hundred frames per minute, and the result is comprehensible, the eye and the brain can follow. But in music and speech there's the time-element. Music and speech—they have to finish coming out, finish being heard. So, therefore, we had to build a system of relationships between image and text, *ex novo*. Eisenstein worked with Prokofiev, they worked side by side, Prokofiev and Sergei Mikhailovich wrote music together, but I think that the true language of cinema still hasn't been invented. I mean, not as a living language, like that of the ancient orators or that of all true literature. Sometimes we have an explanatory language, but that's not what it takes. We have good directors, good cameramen, but not good screenwriters. And I myself wasn't a good screenwriter. With Kuleshov and his collective, I remember, I wrote the script for a film called *By the Law*, adapted from a Jack London story. The shift from the literary work to the film was interesting. The story is about a group of gold prospectors. They're about to set off, one of them is missing. When he shows up he shoots at the others. A woman and man are still alive, the woman disarms the assailant. The three get stuck in the cabin because of a snowstorm, the man and woman want to kill the assassin, but they think he should be tried first. And since they're cut off from the world they try him themselves and then they hang him. We made a good film out of it, but what did we have to do? From the start there were technical problems, we had an extremely reduced budget, so the snowstorm was substituted with the Moskva, which, since it was spring, was thawing. Moreover, we didn't want to content ourselves with the text of the story. I began to think: why did that man shoot them? So we presented him as a laborer hired by the prospectors. He'd found the gold, and the bosses wanted to take it for themselves. In short, it was attempted robbery. There wasn't much text in the film. I wanted the man to escape, tear off the rope. How to show, then, that he realizes he's still alive? Here's what I did: the man is on the ground, passed out, and suddenly he opens his eyes and sees these ants on the ground next to him. Since ants aren't associated with either death or eternal life, the man realizes he's alive. The film was a success, people liked it. It was an ongoing experiment with a cinema built on a minimal number of characters, hardly any exteriors. We filmed with enormous limitations. Things went very well with Kuleshov because his cinema was based on psychological action. So I wrote the script for the *Third Bourgeois*. Abram Room directed it. The film had an odd destiny. I had originally titled it *Triple Love*. In Germany they called it *Basements of Moscow*. Just think, not too long ago I was in East Germany and I saw that film was still being shown. Put on by a women's organization. In France, apparently, it elicited a reply in René Clair's *Under the Roofs of Paris*. In that film there was the story of a three-way relationship, a new formulation of the problem of the love triangle. There's a working-class family, a husband and wife. An old friend of the husband's comes over because he can't find a place to stay. When the husband goes out of town— you can fill in the rest. Then the husband comes back, the wife is with the other guy, but the husband doesn't know where to go; he builds houses, but he has nowhere to live. The woman ends up leaving both men. Even though she's pregnant and doesn't know by whom.

*I haven't seen that film, Viktor Borisovich, but I can see why it would have been screened at a women's organization. It was a prophetic film, ahead of its time on certain topics, certain ideas . . .*

As I've written elsewhere, I think that film anticipated many of the films made later in Europe, films based not on major events, but on everyday private life. When it came out here it raised lots of controversy and I was criticized quite harshly.

*And the film that's remained closest to your heart?*

I wrote the script for *Minin and Pozharsky*. A sensational fiasco. The film was directed by Pudovkin. Of course, if a film doesn't do well, the writer always blames the director . . . Anyway, I loved that script. I knew the characters well, I had studied the source materials exhaustively. I loved the character of Pozharsky. He was a wonderful scribe. And a good historian. He loved music, he would invite *skomorokhs* over. A Dutchman who knew him—I found this tidbit somewhere—wrote that if Russia had been an educated country like Finland or Holland, that man would have had a retinue of musicians singing his praises. He died in virtual oblivion. But he was a true historian. I wanted to make him into a kind of "Idiot" like Prince Myshkin. The director told me: Your Minin and Pozharsky are like members of the government, of the Politburo. You don't know what to make of them. They can't be offended or refuted. Anyway, I liked that idea, but nothing came of it.

*And what relationship do you have with the cinema now?*

Now I don't write scripts anymore, but I must say that I know them. I'll tell you a story. There was a screenwriting contest. I was on the jury (the judges were paid). I read them fast, very fast; one screenwriter saw me speeding through his work and he complained to the minister, who called me in. I tell the screenwriter: "Open the script to page X, and start to read, you'll see that there's a dog or a cat." He tells me there isn't. I say, "Go on, it's there." Astonished, he says: "How did you remember that?" Because, I told him, at that point in the action you all write the same thing. Ah, yes, it's hard to write a good script, and even I, as I've already said, don't consider myself a good screenwriter.

*Who do you like out of the contemporary directors?*

I like Fellini. I like Pasolini, especially that wonderful film where he was able to depict the Gospel with so much freedom of vision. I've also seen other films of his, but they didn't leave as much of an impression.

*And among the Soviet directors of today? In Italy right now people are talking a lot about Tarkovsky.*

I saw his *Rublev*. I didn't like it. I'll explain why. I know Russian history pretty well. And a little about Rublev too. You see, for Rublev to emerge, Rublev's art, there had to be a certain climate, culture. And in fact, Rublev had some friends, he was well known and respected, he was probably paid well. In subsequent eras, a good painter of icons occupied the seat of honor at the tsar's table. And that story about them poking artisans' eyes out so that they could never build a more beautiful monument . . . That's a universal legend, an extremely widespread legend about the construction of churches. Also, it seems to me that Tarkovsky doesn't know ancient Russian art so well. The Russian churches from that period didn't have smooth walls, they didn't use plumb lines yet. And it's precisely the roughness of the walls that gives them their characteristic sense of mass, of massive solidity. But Tarkovsky's churches all have smooth walls, as if they were marble, they look like the walls of the Moscow metro. No, that's not what they were like. And that matters a great deal. I'm talking about the sense, the flavor of an epoch. And then the abundance of horrors . . . You see, at that time in Russia, quartering was not practiced. But that's not all. The Russia of that time, Russia before the Tatar invasion, was a relatively cultured country. The constructions we still have from that time don't at all seem the work of primitives. And Rublev—he was a great school unto himself, with his own vision of the world, with his own systems, his own perspective, a uniquely precise ability to distill and reveal his principal figures. Yes, of course, the problem of the freedom of the artist . . . Rublev was a man surrounded by glory. Even if an artist, I think, always has a hard life. Almost always. Especially when he's good.

*From 1926–30 you wrote the scripts for nineteen films. Subsequently, as of now, you've written only seven others, with huge intervals between. What was your reason for virtually giving up all work in the cinema?*

Because by then, in film, I had done too much.

*You got sick of it?*

No, we got thrown out of that too. I was associated with
Eisenstein. As I told you, in the early days of cinema I had
gone into it reluctantly, but then it grew on me, I became
passionate about it. Some students came out, there was a
little cove of formalists. You know, it's like when you add
a pinch of yeast. And some positions, by then, had been
taken over. Ah, I've got some strange stories about the
cinema. One time, a director, Mikhail Kalatozov, shot a
film from a script written by Tretyakov. It was called *Salt
for Svanetia*. The film didn't pass the censors, they told the
director not to come back. He asked me for help. I went to
the office that handled those things and proposed reedit-
ing the film. They replied that there were no more funds
available. "Twenty-five rubles, would that be possible,
at least?" I asked. They acceded. I watched the film and
re-edited it. You know what the editing consisted of? I
simply took out five hundred meters of film, and with the
director's consent, added another five hundred that were
completely neutral. That is, I added some extra frames so
that the viewer wouldn't have trouble following the pace.
When they saw it again, the film passed, and it was shown

to great success. But I hadn't changed anything, I'd just taken out five hundred meters of film.

*First the "problems," as you call them, with literature, and then with cinema. Allow me to ask a slightly personal question: what did you live on after you left cinema?*

I had put aside some money from my film work. I also wrote articles—you can see my bibliography for yourself, I don't remember, what did I write after the cinema? Articles, reader's reports, lots of them . . . And anyway, you know, there's another peculiar job—writing things for someone else. I have created a few writers that way. One time, for example, I wrote for a very important writer. Here, this is called "revising" a text. I was asked to "revise" this person. He sent me a stack of papers. I read them, then I sat down and wrote the book. It was translated into fourteen languages . . . Of course, life isn't easy . . .

*Yes, I've seen your bibliography, you've really written about all kinds of things: prose, poetry, film, painting, scripts, cars. And you've written novels, literary theory, scripts, essays. You've also written other people's books. Is there anything,*

*Viktor Borisovich, which you haven't done in your life?*

Yes, there's one thing, actually two things, that I've never written: poetry and denunciations.

## December 30

TOLSTOY BEGINS TO WRITE. "A HISTORY OF YESTERDAY."
FOR SOME REASON SHKLOVSKY TORE UP THE FIRST VOL-
UME OF TOLSTOY'S *COMPLETE WORKS*. THE YOUNG TOL-
STOY LEFT FOR THE CAUCASUS WITH AN ENGLISH DIC-
TIONARY, A FLUTE, *THE COUNT OF MONTE CRISTO*, AND
A SAMOVAR. AN ANCESTOR OF OURS LEFT OUT OF *ZOO,
OR LETTERS NOT ABOUT LOVE*. FRIGHTENING, POETIC
DREAMS. WHAT DOES REALISM MEAN?

*Italian readers have recently had the opportunity to read
your monograph on Tolstoy, a writer who, to you, as you
told me one day, feels like a contemporary. A writer who
has kept you company for fifty years, without ever boring
you, you also said. If today you were to resume, in a completely free and "familiar" way, your discussion of Tolstoy,
where would you start?*

From the beginning. From his first work. There's a Tolstoy text that rarely gets published, "A History of Yesterday." In the so-called "Jubilee" edition of Tolstoy, it's included in the first volume. And it is, or was, considered the literal account, in diary form, of Tolstoy's visit to the Bolkonsky estate in 1851—if you want I could even tell you the date, March 24, but these are unimportant details. Actually, "A History of Yesterday" isn't just Tolstoy's first work, even earlier than *Childhood*; it is also a great literary invention, a revelation. Someone, Tolstoy (who in that period was clearly under Sterne's influence), says he wants to record his every thought, to the letter, and along with them the thoughts of those around him; but, for a book of that sort, he goes on, all the ink in the world wouldn't be enough ... In the manuscript version, the text takes up twenty-six pages of a large format notebook. The pages were torn out of the notebook and remained in that state, they were never retranscribed in a clean copy; yet, see, this is a great revelation, great and at the same time premature. But I must tell you something strange: if I cite anything from that text of Tolstoy's, I'd ask you to check it. Because, though I own the Jubilee edition of Tolstoy, the first volume is torn up. Not all the way, but the pages are quite ruined. I have no idea what state I was in the day I did that to it. Undoubtedly in a state of madness. At one time, you must know, I had an impulsive, furious disposition, I often got into street fights and so on . . . But back to the "History." What does Tolstoy write? A young man goes to visit a woman he is enamored with. Her husband comes home, the woman says something about the young man, in French, in the third person. He wishes he could understand: what does this mean, translated into Russian? Is it utterly impolite, or very intimate? When the woman's husband asks him to stay for dinner, he replies by saying his evening is completely full. But as he says these words, his body sits down in a chair and places his hat on the floor. His conscience intervenes at this point, saying: "Well, what are we going to do?" And the young man begins conversing neutrally with the husband. That is, there begins a double, triple discourse: of the conscience, the body, and the subconscious. Then he returns home. And he analyzes the nature of dreams. Tolstoy says we're the ones who make up our dreams, and that they're nothing but our desires. In the morning, when we get out of bed, we create the dreams that we have later. Yes, "A History of Yesterday" is a too little known work. My dear friend, get the book from the library and cite a few passages, it's truly worth the trouble . . .

*Certainly, but in the meantime, we can speak from memory. Tolstoy claims he wants to analyze the* zadushevnaya *element of human behavior. The dictionary translates this word as "intimate," but perhaps there's more to it . . .*

Yes, of course, and I understand that word as *dodushevnaya*, i.e., preceding the soul. In spoken, colloquial Russian, we say that a conversation is *zadushevnaya* to say that it's sincere, heartfelt, uninhibited, but when you have that sort of conversation with yourself, then it's not so much frank and intimate as it is "before the soul."

*So, we have the notion of the subconscious.*

Essentially, "A History of Yesterday" is an attempt to analyze and explain subconscious mechanisms, to explain our chains of decisions. Lev Nikolayevich believed that people choose which thoughts to apply to the decisions they've made. That is, first they decide something and then they ask themselves: why did I make that decision? In this respect, he anticipated the psychological novel—take, for example, *Crime and Punishment*. The problem isn't *what* Raskolnikov thinks, but *why* Raskolnikov thinks it. What is behind or comes before his thoughts.

*You said that the "History" is a revelation as great as it is premature. Perhaps that why it was left unfinished?*

Tolstoy didn't finish writing the "History of Yesterday" because he suddenly decided to leave for the Caucasus. He left abruptly, on foot, as if cast off by life. Tolstoy, at that time, was a big gambler, a young man who loved gypsy women and who had squandered half of his fortune. In Yasnaya Polyana he met his older brother, Nikolai, who was going to the Caucasus, and he tagged along. Nikolai Nikolayevich Tolstoy was an excellent writer who died without having written much of anything, but the little that he did leave behind, like "Hunting in the Caucasus," is wonderful. Lev Nikolayevich said of him that he had a huge flaw that kept him from being a writer: he was too good of a person. When his brother—Tolstoy, the great Tolstoy—arrived, he'd just abandoned university. He studied poorly and rarely. To tell the truth, Lobachevsky, who was rector of the University of Kazan at the time, had noticed that young man, he'd said he was a person with great thoughts. And thus Tolstoy lived happily without working or going to school. And here in Russia, people who don't know what to do with themselves go to the Caucasus. People still went into exile in the Caucasus: Lermontov, Odoevsky, Pushkin himself. When he was there, in the Caucasus, some soldiers asked him if something bad had happened, if he was unhappy—why was he—Count Tolstoy—wearing a humble soldier's uniform? But he wasn't unhappy. He was confused. He had thoughts "before the soul." He wanted to write about what hadn't yet matured in the conscience of man. So, he decided to leave. When he left he took the big notebook where he had begun writing "A History of Yesterday." But the pages he had already written, he ripped them out and left them at home. He took his English dictionary, because he loved Sterne, and his flute, because he wanted to learn how to play. And his brother says to him: Leva, you're a lost cause. You'll never learn English or the flute. Lev Nikolayevich did learn English—the flute, no, even if he continued to study music, from a theoretical point of view. He was an incredible man, he possessed that incredible energy of delusion. Tolstoy wanted to explain what men hide from themselves. He doesn't believe men, what they say. So, for example, in *War and Peace*, he doesn't believe it was Arkady who seduced Natasha. He thinks, and moreover, he wrote it too, that Natasha likes making love. And therefore, she would have been corrupted regardless. Of course, she's confused, she tries to find justifications. But her subconscious is another matter.

*And to what extent, in your opinion, did Tolstoy really succeed in explaining what man hides from himself?*

Sometimes he did succeed. In *War and Peace*, it's not a war in which men decide or think anything. Well, yes, they do think and decide some things, but it's different. There's Napoleon who thinks something, and Davout thinks the same thing, but then Davout suddenly takes pity on the man who was accused of setting the fire in Moscow, an armed man in disguise. And then he forgets having done so. And Pierre goes to jail, and goes as if he's heading to freedom, because everything has already been taken from him and finally he is truly himself. Tolstoy writes about the war and since he experienced two of them (in the Caucasus and in Sevastopol), he wants to show that everybody lies, that everything actually happens in a different way. Tolstoy admired Stendhal for how he represented Waterloo. For the fact that the protagonist, after the battle, no longer knows if he was really at Waterloo or not. Tolstoy discovers that the world is driven by unconscious desires. And he wants to shake people and say, "Stop, return to your selves, wake up!" But everyone keeps following their unconscious paths, even today. But this doesn't mean that the problems of humanity can be resolved with Freud. Freud explains everything with the fact that, for example, a man needs a woman, or another man, but I'm convinced that even the most instinct-driven monkey can't be reduced to just that. He also lives for the fact that he can jump on the trees, that he can express himself through his actions. You know, something happened once that I saw with my own eyes, I was going to put it in *Zoo*, but then I never did. A monkey was locked in a room and they hung some fruit high up on the wall. Underneath it, there was a crate. If he turned the crate on its side, the monkey could almost reach the fruit. But to get it, he would also have to use another crate, which was next to the first. He would have to stack them on top of each other. But he would also have to be sure to put the second crate lengthwise, otherwise it wouldn't have been tall enough. And that monkey, our

175

distant ancestor, did everything right. But when he got the fruit, he was so excited he threw it all over himself. He was inspired. He didn't just want to eat, he wanted to create. What I mean is that, man, since primordial times, has the desire to express himself. One shouldn't believe that man only thinks about sex.

*But, Viktor Borisovich, it's not as if Freud puts it exactly in those terms . . .*

Yes, but what I'm trying to say is that man doesn't only think about fulfilling his desires, but also about fulfilling himself. You see, "A History of Yesterday" can be read according to the Freudian triple schema: language, dream, dream analysis. But Tolstoy didn't continue down that path. On the other hand, though, all the heroes in his works dream. I don't know . . . in, for example, *Anna Karenina*, Anna dreams certain details that are later repeated at her suicide: the old man working at the rails along the platform, muttering to himself . . . Or thinking of another of Tolstoy's early works, the story "The Snowstorm," a singular work written exquisitely by a young writer. The story is this: master and servants go out in a *telega*, and they get lost during a snowstorm. It's very Russian. The nobleman is afraid, whereas the serfs bicker, tell stories. They don't know the art of fear, they don't have the means. But the nobleman, who is Tolstoy, falls asleep and dreams he kisses one of the peasant's hands. Well, what he's seeing is nothing but a citation of Pushkin's *The Captain's Daughter*, when Pugachev expects Grinyov to kiss his hand. That dream contains all the noble Tolstoy's thoughts on the people, on the complexity of his relationship with the people, on the terrible revolution to come—because Pugachev's rebellion was very brutal. And all this was in some little dream. Tolstoy's dreams were even better than the peasants', who, in the Bible, end up in prison with Joseph. And, like Joseph, Tolstoy too knew how to interpret dreams. The "terror of Arzamas" is a dream too—Tolstoy knew the revolution would come, and he knew it was inevitable, and he was afraid of it.

*For Tolstoy, therefore, writing was also somehow a way to exorcise these frightening, prophetic dreams?*

Sure, yes, many writers also write to free themselves, to explain the *zadushevnaya* or *dodushevnaya* part of themselves, to try to bring it to maximum clarity, to develop it like a roll of film. Like in Antonioni's stupendous film, where they develop a photo and accidentally discover a crime . . .

*Speaking of Tolstoy, the supreme epitome of realism, it's funny that all that's come up have been dreams, the subconscious . . .*

Tolstoy, certainly, was a great realist, even if I have never been able to tolerate that word. What does realism mean anyway? There are attempts to describe the world in the most precise manner possible, authors who allow themselves to give free rein to their imaginations, to represent their own dreams with verisimilitude . . . One mustn't forget that in Homer's time the *Iliad* was a reality and that, most likely, when chivalric romances were written, many of them were real: think of the exploits of Cortés, who, with just a small army, conquered empires and continents. But, you see, even the word reality . . . In response to Strakhov telling him that Dostoyevsky might have committed a crime or two, Tolstoy urged him to read Dostoyevsky's books more carefully; he said that the more you read him, the more understandable he becomes. For Tolstoy, in short, Dostoyevsky, with all the implausibility of the daily life contained in his works, is real. Even if stories like that would be hard to imagine from another writer. Tolstoy himself, of course, was convinced that what he wrote was realism. Let's put it this way: realism was what they wrote in that epoch, it was the art of Tolstoy's epoch, of the previous century. It was a way like any other to be able to touch reality. Dostoyevsky used to say that 2 x 2 = 4 is good, but 2 x 2 = 5 is even better. Of course, it was a frustrated and slighted man saying this, but 2 x 2 = 5 represents another logic and even nature, sometimes, conceives it that way. But let's go back to our realist and his "History of Yesterday." So, Tolstoy left for the Caucasus, left the pages of the "History" at home, but took with him *The Count of Monte Cristo*, a samovar, his flute, an English dictionary. Isn't that fantastic? Much more fantastic than the fantasies of Don Quixote. And, mind you, Tolstoy went to the Caucasus on the Volga. It would have been better to go through the mountains, follow the path Pushkin took. But he went down the Volga. Of course, it was possible, but it was more difficult. Yes, Tolstoy's relationship with life, with love, is always "before the soul." Often the poet, the writer, is represented as a prophet. What can I say? Analyzing himself as a person who has developed in a particular environment, the artist becomes conscious of this environment at the same time and can foresee the future. Just think: Columbus went to the Americas and found his way back by predicting the direction of the winds. He came back, in other words, with favorable winds. No one knew they were there, they blew but nobody knew it and all this—understanding, foreseeing, predicting—is very difficult. Einstein said that imagination is stronger than reality, because imagination is the place where anything can happen, whereas in reality there are only obstacles, even if Einstein himself removed not a few of these obstacles. The poet doesn't remove obstacles but creates new paths to get from one place to another.

# January 2

THE WORD. POETRY OF WORDS AND POETRY OF LETTERS.
MAYAKOVSKY LOVED THE RADIO. AN UGLY, STUPID BOX.
ONE MUSTN'T FEAR THE FUTURE. TOLSTOY GETS EDITED.
THE OLD SCHOLASTICISM AND THE NEW. THE LIVING
RUSSIAN WORD.

*In our conversation a few days ago you said that "man lives
in the world, but first and foremost he lives in the world of
words." What do you say we talk today about the funda-
mentally unknown object that is the word?*

In the beginning, there was the word. It was probably a
declaration. Or a cry. Or perhaps a song, because it's been
proven that not only do birds sing, monkeys sing as well,
and this, evidently, brings them some sort of pleasure. It
was when man began to hear, to feel the word, that he

created poetry. And since then he has tried to hold on to it, fix it, remember it. We know nothing about Homer. All we know is that that he was old and blind. He couldn't see and he loved to remember, with precision. Homer lived for *slovesnost*. At the time letters, signs, existed, but literary creation scorned them. Want to know something? In ancient Greece, during trials, everybody had to speak. And if somebody wasn't capable, he would be taught, for example the injured party would have his speech written and then would recite it. It is not up to me to explain how, when, and why letters came into being, but I think that Plato and all the great men of Greece didn't care for *pismenost*. Plato and Socrates fought against written verse. All the great lyric poetry and great drama of ancient Greece is vocal in nature. The Greek world knew how to speak, the Roman as well. As Tyutchev says,

> Blessed is he who visits this life
> at its fateful moments of strife:
> the all-wise sent him an invitation
> to speak with them at their celebrations.

I think in the Greek theater a mistake in the actor's recitation elicited scornful laughter. They liked the word spoken slowly, they loved hearing it. But then, just look at an author closer to us in time, like Shakespeare. To pull Gloucester out of despair, Edgar tells him that down there, far away, there's the sea, and he jumps into this nonexistent sea. But the man talking to Gloucester doesn't correct him. He tells him he fell from the dread summit of a chalky cliff. And this scene didn't provoke laughter in Shakespeare's theater. He knew his public. The word, faith in the word was stronger than the evidence. People didn't marvel that Gloucester believed in the words and that a verbal change in circumstances could be as strong as one in real circumstances. Take Plato, I was looking for the *Phaedo* but I came upon a different dialogue. And I found a very interesting passage. "There is poetry, which, as you know, is complex and manifold. All creation or passage of non-being into being is poetry or making, and the processes of all art are creative; and the masters of arts are all poets or makers." Art, therefore, is the passage from non-being to being . . . but how does this passage occur? For the ancient Greeks this bridge was the word, the well-constructed word, conversation, debate. Yes, I'm very fond of their principles of debate.

*Which goes back to the notion of art as the collision of structures . . .*

Certainly, at the root of poetry there's not just the principle of repetition: the individual lines correspond, but, in a certain way, through this correspondence, they fight with one another. Think of the stanza in *Onegin*, where each verse is a world that enters into conflict with the one that precedes it and where many of the final lines actually parody the rest of the entire stanza. I think that even in the Bible each book fights with the others. There are multiple versions of the discovery of Christ's body. And this can be explained by the fact that the Gospels were initially oral legends, and the differences, therefore, depend on the particular idiom of each legend's place of origin . . . Art creates worlds that materialize, that enter into being, through conflict. But then the problem arises: how do we hold on to them, fix them? Plato, in the *Phaedo*, talks about the essence of this process of retention. Socrates doesn't recognize writing as a great invention—for him it would virtually be comparable to the discovery of chess. That is, man has to speak: it's his pride, his right. And this is where philosophy comes from. It wasn't born in a room, within four walls. Philosophy was born on the street. In ancient Greece, all the doors opened toward the outside, toward the street, before opening them they would knock so they didn't accidentally hit anyone passing by. Yes, poetry knocks before it opens the door to the world and starts a debate. And then came writing. The word "calligraphy" contains *kallós*, which means beauty, but also order, structure. Letters became art because they were beautiful. And, of course, we all love ancient manuscripts, we recognize the love, the care of those who prepared them. And then came the printing press, typography. Even the pages of incunabula are wonderful, like abstract art objects, a union of white, gray, and black. But I think that poetry, the art of the living word, has suffered a great deal from that great invention, the printing press. Letters have completely conquered literature, which has gone from *slovesnost* to *pismenost*. A poetry of letters emerged, poetry started to become calligraphy, and, above all, it became more silent.

*In one of our conversations you said that every innovator is also an "archaist." These words of yours come to mind along with, once again, Russian Cubo-Futurism, where innovation also passes through the recuperation of a sort of "pre-typographical" phase of poetry. I'm thinking of Khlebnikov's love of ancient manuscripts, the very "anti-typographical" structure of some Cubo-Futurist publications, in addition to, of course, the function of the voice, the strong sense of speech in Mayakovsky's lyrics, which, one could say, didn't even knock on the door before going out into the street but flung it open, often hitting passersby . . .*

Yes, Khlebnikov would spend his last cent (and he never had much money) on an antique manuscript. And Mayakovsky was the only poet in the world, I believe, to say:

> Listen,
> comrades of prosperity,
> to the agitator,
> the rabble-rouser.
> Stifling
> the torrents of poetry,
> I'll skip
> the volumes of lyrics;
> as one alive,
> I'll address the living.

Mayakovsky loved the voice in poetry. He wrote his poems not to be read, but for the voice. Yes, he tore verse from the printed page. For example, Volodya loved the radio. With Mayakovsky and the other Futurists, the word became queen again, not only of literature, but of all art.

*Besides the Futurists' explosive return to the "word as such," to me it seems that throughout the Russian poetic tradition of this century there exists a sort of cult of "vocality." A particular "ritual" of declaiming poetry on the part of the poets themselves, experienced as a primal moment in the relationship between poet and audience, and which, for its quality and scale, is without parallel in, for example, the Italian poetic tradition, or Western poetry in general.*

I remember how Blok used to declaim. He would recite his verses as if they were written on the wall. Slow, uninflected. He spoke magnificently. Pasternak too. And Mandelstam lived in the realm of poetry being born, poetry that had just been uttered. Each line gives birth to the next, one by one, and they're all legitimate children. It's too bad they have to be killed. They have to be printed . . . Ah, if only people understood that the birth of poetry is itself poetry. The structuralists, unfortunately, came to the knowledge of art from literature, from "letters." Not from the sound, but the grammar. But the word fixed on the page has another time, it never disappears, a stanza stays right there before your eyes, but its recital lives only in memory. Those are absolutely different things.

*You yourself, as you told me one day, like speaking better than writing.*

Speaking, without question. Debate. You know, I've been a raving orator, tirelessly polemical. The living word . . . like the stupid, ugly square box I work for so often and that really amuses me . . .

*Do you watch television, Viktor Borisovich?*

No, I don't. I just like talking about it. It's another way to unite gesture and word. It has other rules for representing the past, other times. For example, we know that in the theater you can't leave characters hanging over an intermission. In television you can. In written literature, you could even choose not to describe a person, a landscape. These elements also exist in film, you see them, and in television as well. And since it's to be found in everyone's house, it's also to be found in everyone's consciousness. I don't mean to say that now people talk like they do in TV commercials, just as sometimes people speak or write journalistically. But in the battle between newspapers and television, anyway, I'm for TV: at least there, there's the living, spoken word, the sound of the word.

*But don't you think, seeing that this "box" is, by now, in every consciousness, that it's guilty—guiltier than newspapers precisely insofar as it possesses the allure of the spoken, of live sound—of a negative and irreversible linguistic leveling?*

This is a very serious issue, you see. Of course, children watch it and they get their language directly from the television screen. And thus their linguistic upbringing, their wonderful semantic errors, the wonderful "transgression" Khlebnikov talked about, are disappearing. By now, anyway, television can't be taken out of daily life. Perhaps one day people will say: before television and after television, just as today we say: before cinema and after cinema. That beautiful thing that is dialect will disappear, the complex variety of individual languages will vanish. Here in Russia, every village speaks a different language. Of course, this is a problem that must be reflected on. The new means of communication certainly represent a loss, a loss in creativity. But one needn't be afraid of technology. At one time people were afraid of trains, they thought that rail traffic was going to cause horrible catastrophes. But people ought to love the future.

*But I was talking about language, Viktor Borisovich. And, I could also respond with the wisecrack that I definitely can't imagine Anna Karenina dead beneath a television.*

Yes, it's right to be afraid for language. Because, on top of that, they don't know how to do things right in that little box. For example, our age, our literary consciousness has already developed the compositional techniques of the screenplay in an extremely refined way. But instead they show endless police series that are extremely weak precisely from the point of view of the script's composition. They're scripts without conflicts. Or rather, the conflict is always a transgression of the law: "man and law," as we call them in Russia. Someone commits a crime, someone else finds a solution to the crime. Whereas literature reached *Crime and Punishment* over a century ago. It reached the point of asking: what is transgression really? . . . Yes, this box slips into our consciousness, but . . . but then I should say something else too: Today, in such a turbulent time in history, we can't occupy ourselves with creating all this scientific terminology, either . . . Look, if we take a book on linguistics, a structuralist book—I do have them, you see, I'm not unaware of them—they're written in another language, a language they created in which only structuralists can express themselves. It's jargon. Not a language.

*How can a language be created? Who creates it?*

Let me put it this way: Gogol's language is more the language of language. But it's language. Tolstoy's language is language. How do I know? Simple. When I turn in my book manuscripts to publishing houses, every time I quote from Tolstoy I always write "Tolstoy" in the margin. Otherwise the proofreader or editor would undoubtedly change some of the words. And when Tolstoy was alive, with all the respect everyone had for him, they would make up to two thousand edits in one book. And the editor was certainly no idiot. The fact is that Tolstoy wrote in the language of the future, in the language to come. Whereas the editor wasn't even writing in the language of the present, but the language of the past. Khlebnikov, with his whole mystical approach to language, also lived in the living language. But no one can live in a non-language, no one can live in a no-man's language. The language of professors is always ugly . . . In Russia, when we were under tsarism, there was a special theater commission, composed of famous second-rate professors. They were executioners who tortured the body of Chekhov's work. And today we find ourselves facing a new scholasticism—though, don't get me wrong, scholasticism had its place—which is a branch that has broken off the tree, a fruitless branch. We need to concern ourselves with the creation of new living language, and not with conventional jargon. In chemistry, for example, when they discover a new element they give it a name; in language, we don't create new phenomena, we give new names to old phenomena.

*And what is the destiny of these new names? Why do some words die out and others come into being?*

Words become tedious. Or they become dull like knives with overused blades. Or they become sacred.

*One last, direct question: in your opinion, which poet or which writer from this century has done the most for the Russian language, for the living Russian word?*

More than anyone, Khlebnikov, who has still not been read thoroughly enough. The lesson to be learned from Khlebnikov's prose hasn't yet come to fruition, but its time will come, and writers will be reading him.

# Notes

p. 28    *GPU*: State Political Directorate (*Gosudarstven-noye Politicheskoye Upravlenie*), Soviet Union secret police from 1922–1934.

p. 29    *Dantonesque*: reference to Georges Danton, statesman and leader of the French Revolution whose booming voice was legendary.

p. 55    *Thackeray*: Though Shklovsky names Thackeray, this refers to Sir Walter Scott's *The Tale of Old Mortality* (1816) where the narrator, having decided against writing a conclusion to his novel, is questioned by a friend during tea: "'Really, madam,' said I, 'you must be aware that every volume of a narrative turns less and less interesting as the author draws to a conclusion,—just like your tea, which, though excellent hyson, is necessarily weaker and more insipid in the last cup. Now, as I think the one is by no means improved by the luscious lump of half-dissolved sugar usually found at the bottom of it, so I am of opinion that a history, growing already vapid, is but dully crutched up by a detail of circumstances which every reader must have anticipated, even though the author exhaust on them every flowery epithet in the language."'

Shklovsky makes occasional errors of this sort throughout the text.

p. 61   *veiki*: In Finnish, *veikko* means friend, brother, or fellow; in Petersburg, the term *veiki* was used to refer to both the drivers as well as the carriage.

p. 61   *funt*: Russian pound (409.5 grams), now obsolete.

p. 62   *Moscow does nothing, Petersburg creates nothing*: Paraphrase of a passage in Belinsky's "Petersburg and Moscow" in *Fiziologiya Peterburga* (The Physiology of Petersburg). "The inhabitant of Petersburg is eternally sick with the fever of reality; frequently he in reality does nothing [*delaet nichego*], in contradistinction to the inhabitant of Moscow, who doesn't do anything [*nichego ne delaet*], but the 'nothing' of the inhabitant of Petersburg for himself is always 'something.'" (Translation courtesy of Tom Dolack.)

p. 62    *distinguished places of presence and absence*: The now-obsolete term *prisutstvennoe mesto*, literally "place of presence," indicated the public offices where important meetings and assemblies were held, and by extension the places where power was exercised. Hence the play on words.

p. 65    *Vladimir*: A high military decoration in pre-revolutionary Russia.

p. 73    *Hylaea*: the name of the original Cubo-Futurist group.

p. 73    *"stone women"*: known as kurgan stelae, an ancient form of grave monument in the form of anthropomorphic stone slabs (which in Russia usually depicted women).

p. 73   *Khlebnikov's grave at the Aleksandr Nevsky cemetery*: his grave is actually in Moscow's Novodevichy Cemetery.

p. 79   *like Mendeleev's*: Mendeleev created the periodic table of elements.

p. 89   *Karamzinists*: followers of Nikolai Karamzin (1766–1826), writer and historian. At the turn of the nineteenth century, they clashed with the followers of Admiral Shishkov (1753–1841) (Shiskovites) who supported strict linguistic conservatism.

p. 89   *Hermann and Raskolnikov*: Protagonists of Pushkin's "The Queen of Spades" and Dostoyevsky's *Crime and Punishment*, respectively.

p. 85   *"I have forgotten* [. . .]": lines from Osip Mandelstam, *Tristia* No. 113.

p. 90   *Akaky*: Akaky Akakievich Bashmachkin, protagonist of Gogol's "The Overcoat."

p. 90   *In the very name Akaky*: the literal meaning of the name, derived from the Greek, meaning "harmless" or "lacking evil," suggests the extent of humiliation it must have taken to drive the ghost to violence.

p. 92   *Golyadkin*: protagonist of Dostoyevsky's *The Double*.

p. 92   *shed tears over a work of imagination*: from Pushkin's "Elegy" (1930).

p. 93   *Yudenich was approaching Petrograd*: Nikolai Nikolaevich Yudenich (1862–1933), tsarist general and commander of the White Army. His attack on Petrograd, in 1919 during the Russian Civil War, failed.

p. 95   *Sverdlov*: Yakov Sverdlov (1885–1919), a political official and Bolshevik leader, was elected chairman of the Central Executive Committee in 1917.

p. 107     *Mont de Piété*: name of an institutional pawnbro-
ker organization in Europe from the fifteenth to
twentieth centuries.

p. 109     *Kornilov*: Lavr Kornilov (1870–1918), tsarist army
general, became Supreme Commander-in-Chief
of the army in July 1917. A month later, he spear-
headed an attempted coup d'état. Shortly there-
after, he helped to establish the Volunteer Army,
which fought against the Bolsheviks in the Civil
War. He died in battle.

p. 110     *SRs*: Acronym that stands for Socialist-Revolutionary Party.

p. 112     *byliny*: Russian folk epics.

p. 113     *Sviatoslav*: A Kievan prince who was decapitated
by his enemies. He appears as a character in
Khlebnikov's "Otter's Children."

p. 113     *valenki*: traditional Russian boots made of wool
felt.

p. 132  *Potemkin villages*: the famous "façades" of pros-
perous villages that Potemkin had ordered constructed in the country to impress the empress
when she came to visit.

p. 137  *Krug*: "circle" in Russian.

p. 137  *Malyar*: "painter" in Russian.

p. 138  *poka chto*: for now, for the time being, while, as
long as.

p. 138  *nichego*: the literal meaning of *nichego* is "nothing"; colloquially, it is often used as an adverb to
mean: "not bad," "pretty good," or "so-so."

p. 156  *Chapayev*: famous film by the Vasilyev brothers
adapted from Dmitri Furmanov's eponymous
novel.

p. 160  *Third Bourgeois*: distributed as *Bed and Sofa* in
Anglophone countries.

p. 161   *Minin and Pozharsky*: Kozma Minin (a meat trader) and the prince Dmitry Pozharksy banded together to lead the Volunteer Army that, in September 1612, drove out the Polish forces occupying Moscow, thus putting an end to foreign occupation and the "Time of Troubles."

p. 161   *skomorokhs*: street performers, traveling players in Medieval Russia.

p. 182   *slovesnost*: both *slovesnost* and, later on, *pismenost*, have the same general meaning as "literature." But whereas the former derives from *slovo*, word, the latter derives from *pismo*, graphic sign or writing.

The translator would like to thank Tom Dolack and Katya Hokanson, as well as Serena Vitale, for their invaluable assistance with all matters Russian.

# Glossary of Names

AKHMATOVA, ANNA ANDREYEVNA, pseudonym of Anna Andreyevna Gorenko (1889–1966). Poet; initially a member of the Acmeist movement. Her first husband was the poet Nikolay Gumilev. Notable works include "Poem without a Hero" and *Requiem*.

AFANASIEV, ALEKSANDR NIKOLAEVICH (1826–1871). Literary historian and folklorist, representative of the "mythological school." He collected Russian folk tales and published the three-volume work *The Slavs' Poetic Outlook on Nature*.

BABEL, ISAAC EMMANUILOVICH (1894–1940). Writer of works such as *Red Cavalry* and *Odessa Tales*. Arrested in 1939, he died in a gulag.

BAUDOUIN DE COURTENAY, JAN NIECISŁAW (1845–1929). Linguist. Born and educated in Poland, he worked in various foreign universities for much of his life. He established the Kazan School of Linguistics in the mid-1870s.

BELY, ANDREI, pseudonym of Boris Nikolaevich Bugaev (1880–1934). Poet, novelist, and theorist of symbolism. His writings include the novels *The Silver Dove, Petersburg, Kotik Letaev*, and the essay collections *Symbolism* and *The Mastery of Gogol*.

BLOK, ALEKSANDR ALEKSANDROVICH (1880–1921). The great lyric poet of Russian symbolism. His poem "The Twelve" addresses the October Revolution.

BRIK, LILYA (LILI) YURYEVNA (1891–1978). Osip Brik's wife and also Mayakovsky's companion.

BRIK, OSIP MAKSIMOVICH (1888–1945). Literary critic and theorist. An exponent of formalism, he was one of the most active members of *LEF*.

BUKHARIN, NIKOLAI IVANOVICH (1888–1938). Politician. A member of the Bolshevik party, he was in the Politburo from 1919–29 and on the Central Committee from

1917–34. In 1937 he was expelled from the party, tried, and executed.

BULGAKOV, MIKHAIL AFANASYEVICH (1891–1940). Novelist and playwright. His works include *The White Guard*, *Black Snow*, and *The Master and Margarita* (posthumously published).

BURLIUK, DAVID DAVIDOVICH (1882–1967). Painter and poet. He discovered Mayakovsky's poetic talent and through his tenacious organizing consolidated the Cubo-Futurist group. In 1920, he emigrated to Japan, and in 1922 moved to the United States.

DERZHAVIN, GAVRILA ROMANOVICH (1743–1816). Poet. Considered the greatest Russian poet before Pushkin. He is known for his odes, in particular "On the Death of Prince Meschersky," "Ode to Felitsa," and "God."

EIKHENBAUM, BORIS MIKHAILOVICH (1886–1959). Literary theorist and historian. A member of Opoyaz, his works include *Leo Tolstoy, Anna Akhmatova, Literary Mores*.

EISENSTEIN, SERGEI MIKHAILOVICH (1898–1948). Director. Author of renowned films such as *October: The Ten Days that Shook the World*, *The Battleship Potemkin*, *Alexander Nevsky*, *Ivan the Terrible*.

ERENBURG, ILYA GRIGORYEVICH (1891–1967). Writer. Author of, among others, the novel *The Thaw* and the autobiography *People, Years, Life*.

ESENIN, SERGEI ALEKSANDROVICH (1895–1925). Poet. After a period of "peasant" lyric poems, he greeted the revolution in mystical-prophetic terms. He was subsequently a leader of the imagist movement. He committed suicide in a Leningrad hotel room.

FEDIN, KONSTANIN ALEKSANDROVICH (1892–1977). Writer. His books include *Cities and Years*, *The Rape of Europe*, and *Writer, Art, Time*.

FILONOV, PAVEL (1883–1941). Painter and sometime poet. He developed and theorized a style called "analytical realism" or "anti-cubism."

FORSH, OLGA DMITRIEVNA (1873–1961). Writer. Her work includes the roman á clef *The Ship of Fools* depicting the Petrograd House of Arts.

GIPPIUS, ZINAIDA NIKOLAEVNA (1869–1945). Poet, prose writer, and critic. Recognized as one of Russia's most important women writers and something of a dandy. She and her husband Dmitri Merezhkovsky went into exile in 1920.

GORKY, MAXIM, pseudonym of Aleksey Maksimovich Peshkov (1868–1936). Writer. His many works include the novels *Mother* and *The Life of Matvei Kozhemyakin*. After an initial fallout with the Bolsheviks and a long period of residency abroad, he returned to the USSR in 1931.

GURO, ELENA GENRIKHOVNA (1877–1913). Writer, painter, and Cubo-Futurist.

IVANOV, VYACHESLAV IVANOVICH (1886–1949). Symbolist poet. Also a philosopher, literary critic, and translator.

IVANOV, VSEVOLOD VIACHESLAVOVICH (1895–1963).

Writer. His works include the novel *Armoured Train 14-69*.

JAKUBINSKY, LEV PETROVICH (1892–1945). Formalist critic and linguist.

KAMENSKY, VASILY VASILEVICH (1884–1961). Poet and artist associated with Cubo-Futurism. He was also one of the editors of *Vesna*.

KAVERIN, VENIAMIN ALEKSANDROVICH (1902–1989). Writer. A character in his first novel, *Skandalist*, was modeled on Viktor Shklovsky. He also wrote many other works, including the acclaimed *Two Captains*.

KRUCHENYKH, ALEKSEI ELISEEVICH (1886–1969). Poet. Perhaps the most radical member of the Cubo-Futurist group, he wrote the poem "Zaum" and developed the theory of "trans-sense" poetry.

KÜCHELBECKER, WILHELM (1797–1846). Russian Romantic poet and Decembrist. Yury Tynyanov wrote a biography of him called *Kyukhlya*.

Kulbin, Nikolai Ivanovich (1868–1917). Doctor, painter, art theorist. He organized and supported many avant-garde events and publications.

Kuleshov, Lev Vladimirovich (1899–1970). Filmmaker and theorist. His films include *The Extraordinary Adventures of Mr. West in the Land of the Bolsheviks* and *By the Law*.

Lunts, Lev Natanovich (1901–1924). Writer, playwright, and theorist. He wrote the Serapion Brothers' manifesto "To the West!"

Mayakovsky, Vladimir Vladimirovich (1893–1930). Poet and Cubo-Futurist. Merging ideological militancy and literary experimentation, he was at the center of many important initiatives in post-revolutionary Soviet literature. He founded LEF (and the eponymous journal) (1923–25) and the *New LEF* (1927–29). He committed suicide.

Malevich, Kazimir (1878–1935). Painter. A pioneer of abstract art, he originated the Suprematist movement.

Mandelstam, Osip Emilevich (1891–1938). Poet and prose writer affiliated with the Acmeists. Arrested for the first time in 1934 and "exiled" to Voronezh, he was again arrested in 1938. He died in a gulag in the Far East.

MATYUSHIN, MIKHAIL (1861–1934). Painter and composer affiliated with the Futurists.

MAYKOV, APOLLON NIKOLAYEVICH (1821–1897). Poet.

MENDELEEV, DMITRI IVANOVICH (1837–1907). Chemist and inventor.

MEREZHKOVSKY, DMITRI SERGEYEVICH (1865–1941). Prose writer and essayist. An exponent of pre-symbolist decadence. An opponent of the Bolshevik regime, he and his wife, Zinaida Gippius, went into exile.

MEYERHOLD, VSEVOLOD EMILEVICH (1874–1940). Theater director. A student of Konstantin Stanislavsky's, he staged innovative and controversial plays. He founded his own theater in 1922, which was closed down in 1938. Arrested in 1939, he was executed by firing squad in 1940. He was later rehabilitated.

NIKITIN, NIKOLAI NIKOLAEVICH (1895–1963). Writer

and member of the Serapion Brothers.

PASTERNAK, BORIS LEONIDOVICH (1890–1960). Poet and prose writer. Initially a member of the "moderate" Futurist group "The Centrifuge" and *LEF* contributor. The controversy over *Doctor Zhivago* provoked such a large-scale campaign of criticisms and accusations that he was expelled from the Writers' Union. He was awarded the Nobel Prize in 1958.

PAVLOV, IVAN PETROVICH (1849–1936). Physiologist.

PYAST (PESTOVSKY), VLADIMIR ALEKSEEVICH (1886–1940). Poet.

POLIVANOV, YEVGENI DMITRIEVICH (1891–1938). Linguist. A member of Opoyaz, in the Thirties he lived in semi-exile in Samarkand and then in Tashkent. Accused of spying for Japan during the Great Purge, he was tried and executed. He was later rehabilitated.

POLONSKAIA, ELIZAVETA GRIGOREVNA (1890–1969). Poet.

POZNER, VLADIMIR ALEKSANDROVICH (1908–1975). Writer. Born in Paris, where he returned in the Twenties after a period in Russia. He is renowned in France as a Russian-French writer and has published several novels and critical works, including translations of some of Viktor Shklovsky's books.

PROKOFIEV, SERGEI SERGEYEVICH (1891–1953). Composer. After fifteen years of voluntary exile in the West, he returned to the USSR permanently in 1933.

PUDOVKIN, VSEVOLOD (1893–1953). Filmmaker. Directed acclaimed films such as *Mother, The End of St. Petersburg,* and *Storm over Asia.*

RAIKH, ZINAIDA NIKOLAEVNA (1898–1939). Actress. She was married to Sergei Esenin and then Vsevolod Meyerhold.

REMIZOV, ALEKSEI MIKHAILOVICH (1877–1957). Writer and artist. Wrote fantastic, horror, and satirical stories and novels. After a brief period in Berlin, he moved to Paris in 1924.

ROOM, ABRAM (1894–1976). Director. After studying with Lev Kuleshov at the State Film School, he became a prolific filmmaker.

SCRIABIN, ALEKSANDR NIKOLAYEVICH (1872–1915). Composer and pianist. Innovative and controversial, he is a major figure among Russian composers.

SEVERYANIN, IGOR VASILYEVICH (Lotarev) (1887–1941). Poet. Founder and principal exponent of Ego-Futurism. One of the first poets to leave Russia after the 1917 Revolution, he moved to Estonia in 1918.

SHAGINYAN, MARIETTA SERGEEVNA (1888–1982). Poet, prose writer, and public activist.

SHOSTAKOVICH, DMITRI DMITRIYEVICH (1906–1975). Composer.

SIMONOV, KONSTANTIN MIKHAILOVICH (1915–1979). Writer. Well-known as a poet, he also wrote acclaimed plays and novels, such as *Days and Nights*.

SLONIMSKY, MIKHAIL LEONIDOVICH (1897–1972). Writer and member of the Serapion Brothers.

SOLZHENITSYN, ALEKSANDR ISAYEVICH (1918–2008). Novelist and historian. Authored major works such as: *The Gulag Archipelago, Cancer Ward, The First Circle, August 1914*, and *One Day in the Life of Ivan Denisovich*. He was awarded the Nobel in 1970. Exiled from the Soviet Union in 1974, he lived in the United States until his return to Russia in 1994.

STANISLAVSKI, KONSTANTIN SERGEYEVICH (1863–1938). Theater director, actor, theater theorist. He, along with Vladimir Nemirovich-Danchenko, founded the Moscow Art Theater.

STRAKHOV, NIKOLAI NIKOLAEVICH (1828–1896). Publicist, philosopher, and literary critic. He wrote biographies of Dostoyevsky and Tolstoy.

TATLIN, VLADIMIR YEVGRAFOVICH (1885–1953). Painter and sculptor. An important artist in the avant-garde and

Constructivism.

TERENTYEV, IGOR GERASIMOVICH (1892–1937). Theater director. Initially a member of the futurist-inspired group 41° founded in Tiflis, Georgia in 1918.

TIKHONOV, NIKOLAY SEMENOVICH (1896–1979). Poet and prose writer. One of the Serapion Brothers, his poems and stories often deal with war.

TRETYAKOV, SERGEI MIKHAILOVICH (1892–1937). Poet, playwright, and literary theorist. He was associated with the Ego-Futurists and involved in the Siberian futurist group Creation founded in the early 1920s. He also contributed to *LEF* and was one of *New LEF*'s editors. He was a victim of the Great Purge but was later rehabilitated.

TYNYANOV, YURY NIKOLAEVICH (1894–1943). Writer and literary theorist. Member of Opoyaz and author of *Archaists and Innovators* and *The Problem of Poetic Language*.

VENGEROV, SEMYON AFANASYEVICH (1855–1920). Literary historian and professor at the University of St. Petersburg.

VERTOV, DZIGA (pseudonym of Denis Arkadievich Kaufman) (1896–1954). Director. In 1922, he founded the "Kino-eye" group and the film journal *Kino-Pravda*. He made acclaimed films such as *One-Sixth of the World* and *Man with a Movie Camera*.

VINOGRADOV, VIKTOR VLADIMIROVICH (1895–1969). Linguist and literary theorist.

ZAMYATIN, YEVGENY IVANOVICH (1884–1937). Writer. An engineer and specialist in naval construction, he lived in England for several years. After returning to Russia in 1917, he took up literature, and is best known for the dystopian satire *We*. He left Russia in 1931.

ZHDANOV, ANDREI ALEKSANDROVICH (1896–1948). Politician. Involved in cultural affairs in close collaboration with Stalin. In 1946, he denounced Akhmatova and Zoshchenko (among others) in his infamous "report."

ZHIRMUNSKY, VIKTOR MAKSIMOVICH (1891–1971). Linguist and literary theorist.

Zoshchenko, Mikhail Mikhailovich (1895–1958). Writer. Author of satirical stories and novels, he was expelled from the Writers' Union in 1946.

# Timeline of Works

Here are the titles (and their English translations) of Viktor Shklovsky's major writings and film scripts. For a
comprehensive list of publications, see Richard Sheldon,
*Viktor Shklovsky: An International Bibliography of Works
by and about Him*, Ann Arbor: Ardis, 1977.

1914    *Svintsovii zhrebii* (*The Lead Die*); *Voskreshenie
        slova* ("Resurrection of the Word," first English
        translation 1972, included in *Theory of Prose*)

1921    *Rozanov* (included in *Theory of Prose* as "Literature
        without a Plot: Rozanov"); *Razvertyvanie siuzheta*
        (*The Unfolding of the Plot*; included in *Theory of
        Prose* as "The Making of *Don Quixote*"); *Tristram
        Shendi Sterna i teoriia romana* (English trans.
        1965, included in *Theory of Prose* as "The Novel
        as Parody: Sterne's *Tristram Shandy*"); *Revoljucija
        i front* ("Revolution and the Front," the first sec-
        tion of *A Sentimental Journey*, see below)

1922 "Epilog" ("Epilogue," which becomes the last section of *A Sentimental Journey*)

1923 *Xod konja* (*Knight's Move*, English translation 2005); *Sentimental'noe puteshestvie* (*A Sentimental Journey*, English translation 1970); *Zoo, ili pis'ma ne o ljubvi* (*Zoo, or Letters Not about Love*, English translation 1971); *Literatura i kinematograf* (*Literature and Cinematography*, English translation 2008)

1925 *O teorii prozy* (*Theory of Prose*, English translation 1990); *Iprit* (Mustard Gas, with Vsevolod Ivanov)

1926 *Tret'ja fabrika* (*Third Factory*, English translation 1977); *Puteshestvie v stranu kino* (A Trip to the Cinema, children's); *Udachi i porazhenija Maksima Gor'kogo* (Maxim Gorky's Successes and Defeats); *A. Xoxlova* (with Sergei Eisenstein)

1927 *Pjat' chelovek znakomyx* (*Five People I Know*); *Texnika pisatel'skogo remesla* (*Technique of the Writer's Trade*, reprinted in 1928, '29, '30); *Ix nastojashchee* (*Their Present*); *Motalka* (*Reels*)

1928    *Mater'jal i stil' v romane L'va Tolstogo "Vojna i mir"* ("Material and Style in Tolstoy's *War and Peace*"); *Nandu II* (children's); *Gamburgskij schet* (*Hamburg Account*, English translation forthcoming 2013); *Kratkaja i dostovernaja povest' o dvorjanine Bolotove* (*The Short but True Story of the Nobleman Bolotov*, children's)

1929    *Room: zhizn' i rabota* (*Abram Room: Life and Work*); *Matvej Komarov: zhitel' goroda Moskvy* (*Matvej Komarov: Citizen of Moscow*)

1930    *Podenshchina* (*Work by Day*); *Gornaja Gruzija* (*Mountain Georgia*); *Turksib* (children's)

1931    *Poiski optimizma* (*A Hunt for Optimism*, English translation 2012); *Marko Polo razvedchik* (*Marco Polo the Spy*, children's); *Skazka o tenjax* (*Tale of the Shadows*; children's), *Kak pisat' scenarii* (*How to Write a Scenario*); "*Kak ustroen avtomobil'*" (*How an Automobile is Made*); *Zhitie arxiereijskogo sluzhi* (*Life of a Bishop's Assistant*, English translation forthcoming, 2014.)

1933   *Chulkov i Levshin* (Chulkov and Levshin)

1934   *Svet v lesu* (*Light in the Forest*); *Belomorsko-Baltijskij kanal imeni Stalina* (with others, edited by Maxim Gorky, English trans. as *Belomor*, 1935)

1936   *Marko Polo* (*Marco Polo*), *Zhizn' xudozhnika Fedotova* (*Life of the Painter Fedotov*, children's

1937   *Rasskaz o Pushkine* (*History of Pushkin*); *Zametki o proze Pushkina* (*Notes on Pushkin's Prose*)

1939   *Dnevnik* (*Diary*)

1940   *O Maiakovskom* (*On Mayakovsky*; English trans. as *Mayakovsky and His Circle*, 1972); *Minin i Pozharskij* (*Minin and Pozharsky*)

1944   *Vstrechi* (*Encounters*)

1951. *O masterax starinnyx* (*On the Ancient Craftsmen*)

1953 *Zametki o proze russkix klassikov* (*Notes on the Prose of the Russian Classics*)

1957 *Za i protiv. Zametki o Dostoevskom* (*Pro and Contra: Notes on Dostoyevsky*)

1958 *Istoricheskie povesti i rasskazy* (*Historical Novellas and Stories*)

1959 *Chudozhestvennaja proza* (*Artistic Prose*)

1963 *Lev Tolstoy* (*Lev Tolstoy*, English translation 1978)

1964 *Zhyli-byli* (*Once upon a Time*)

1965 *Za sorok let* (*Over Forty Years*)

1966 *Staroe i novoe* (*Old and New*); *Povesti o proze* (*Tales of Prose*)

1970   *Tetiva. O nesxodstve sxodnogo* (*Bowstring: On the Dissimilarity of the Similar*, English translation 2011)

1973   *Ejzenshtejn (Eisenstein); Sobranie sochinenij v 3-x tomax, 1973-4. (Works, 3 Vols.)*

1981   *Energiia zabluzhdeniia: kniga o siuzhete* (*Energy of Delusion: A Book on Plot*, English translation 2007)

# Film Scripts

1926   *Krylya kholopa* (*The Wings of a Serf*) with Konstantin Schildkroet and Yuri Tarich; *Po zakonu* (*By the Law*), directed by Lev Kuleshov; *Predatel* (*The Traitor*), with Lev Nikulin, directed by Abram Room

1927   *Schastlivyje cherepki* with Konstantin Derzhavin, directed by Eduard Ioganson; *Tretya meshchanskaya* (*Bed and Sofa*) with Abram Room, and directed by Room; *Evrei na zimle* (*The Jews of the Earth*, documentary), intertitles by Vladimir Mayakovsky, directed by Abram Room

1928   *Dva bronevika* (*The Two Armored Cars*) with Semyon Timoshenko, and directed by Semyon Timoshenko; *Dom na Trubnoy* (*The House on Trubnaya Square*), with Nikolay Erdman, Anatoli Marienhof, Vadim Shershenevich, and Bella

Zorich, directed by Boris Barnet; *Kazaki* (*The Cossacks*), with Vladimir Barsky and directed by Barsky; *Kapitanskaya dochka* (*The Captain's Daughter*), directed by Yuri Tarich; *Molodost pobezhdaet* (*Youth Wins*) with Giorgi Mdvani, directed by Mikhail Gelovani; *Ovod* (*Wisp*) with Kote Mardzhanov, directed by Mardzhanov; *Poslednij attrakcion* (*The Last Attraction*), directed by Olga Preobrazhenskaya

1930    *Amerikanka* (*American Woman*) with Giorgi Mdvani and Giorgi Sturna, directed by Leo Esakya; *Ochen prosto* (*Just Like That*) with Giorgi Mdvani, directed by Grigori Lomidze; *Gorizont* (*Horizon*) with Lev Kuleshov and Georgi Munblit, directed by Kuleshov; *Mertvyi Dom* (*House of the Dead*) with Vasili Fyodorov, directed by Fyodorov

1933    Dialogue for *Zhit* (*Live*), directed by Semyon Timoshenko

1937    *Tri medvedya* (*The Three Bears*, animated), directed by Maria Benderskaya

SERENA VITALE is a professor of Russian language and literature at the Università Cattolica del Sacro Cuore in Milan. She is the author of numerous books and essays on Russian literature, and has also translated many Russian novels into Italian. Her acclaimed biographical work *Pushkin's Button* was translated into English in 1999.

JAMIE RICHARDS is the translator of Giovanni Orelli's *Walaschek's Dream*, Nicolai Lilin's *Free Fall*, and Giancarlo Pastore's *Jellyfish*, among other works.

# SELECTED DALKEY ARCHIVE TITLES

FOR A FULL LIST OF PUBLICATIONS, VISIT:
**www.dalkeyarchive.com**

## SELECTED DALKEY ARCHIVE TITLES

FOR A FULL LIST OF PUBLICATIONS, VISIT:
www.dalkeyarchive.com